AUSTRALIA IN YOUR POCKET

AUSTRALIA
IN YOUR POCKET

A STEP-BY-STEP GUIDE
AND TRAVEL ITINERARY

BY JOHN GOTTBERG

Horizon Books

British Library Cataloguing in Publication Data
Gottberg, John
    Australia in your pocket: a step-by-step guide and
    travel itinerary. — (Pocket travellers).
    1. Australia — Visitors' guides
    I. Title II. Series
    919. 4'0463

    ISBN 1-85461-025-2

This edition first published in 1989 by Horizon Books Ltd,
Harper & Row House, Estover Road, Plymouth PL6 7PZ, United
Kingdom. Tel: Plymouth (0752) 705251. Telex: 45635. Fax: (0752)
777603.

Printed and bound in Great Britain

CONTENTS

How to Use This Book   6
Itinerary   17
Tour 1 Arrive in Sydney   21
Tour 2 Around Sydney   28
Tour 3 More of Sydney   33
Tour 4 Sydney to Canberra   37
Tour 5 Canberra   43
Tour 6 Canberra to Beechworth   47
Tour 7 Beechworth to Melbourne   51
Tour 8 Melbourne   59
Tour 9 Ballarat   65
Tour 10 Dandenong Ranges and Phillip Island   69
Tour 11 Alice Springs   73
Tour 12 Alice Springs to Ayers Rock   78
Tour 13 Ayers Rock   81
Tour 14 Ayers Rock to Wallara Ranch   84
Tour 15 Wallara Ranch to Alice Springs   86
Tour 16 Alice Springs to Cairns   88
Tour 17 Green Island   93
Tour 18 Great Barrier Reef   95
Tour 19 Cairns to Brisbane   98
Tour 20 Brisbane and the Gold Coast   105
Tour 21 The Gold Coast   113
Tour 22 Fly Home from Brisbane   116
Post Tour Options   117
    Tasmania
    Adelaide and South Australia
    Perth and Western Australia
    Darwin and the 'Top End'
    Great Barrier Reef Islands
Holidays and Festivals   140
How to Speak 'Strine'   142

HOW TO USE THIS BOOK

G'day! In your hands is your fair dinkum, pocket-sized Aussie
tour guide. It's designed for independent-minded blokes and birds
who like the freedom and flexibility of going walkabout their own
way, but who appreciate the efficiency that an organised tour
offers.

Australia in Your Pocket doesn't pretend to take you around the
entire continent of 'Oz' in three weeks. That would be like trying
to see the whole United States in that time. It's a fair
comparison: Australia is almost identical in size to the 48
contiguous states.

What I have tried to do in this itinerary is to provide a
sampling of Australia's most fascinating features — from the great
cities of Sydney and Melbourne, to predictable (and worthwhile!)
tourist stops such as the Great Barrier Reef and Ayers Rock, to
less known sites like reconstructed gold rush towns and an island
of nesting penguins—and suggest how to appreciate them most
thoroughly. I have done this in a manner to show how to get the
maximum value for your travel pound.

Because Australia is so vast, in order to see as much as possible
within such an itinerary, you should rely on domestic airlines to
cover large chunks of land between major attractions. Most of
Australia's 16 million people live along the relatively fertile
southeast coast, an area well-equipped with good roads and visitor
facilities. The same is not true of the Outback. To get to the dry
Centre from any direction, you are faced with a journey of many
hundreds of miles across bleak, foreboding terrain. It is probably
not a good idea to drive yourself there. Air travel, while no
bargain, can save considerable time and worry. With extra time,
much of the trip can be done by hire car or (more cheaply and
reliably but with somewhat less freedom) by train and bus.

The trip outlined in this book begins in Sydney and concludes
in Brisbane. I suggest that you take an extra day or two off work
to arrive in Sydney on Saturday morning to begin your adventure.
This will make connections easier later in the trip (especially on
the infrequent Alice Springs – Cairns air leg) and will allow you
some time to recover from jet lag at home before going back to
work when your holiday's finished.

I like to compare any travel plan to a children's Lego set. The
itinerary should provide a framework for travel, but should not
restrict the wanderer from indulging personal interests or whims.
Take this itinerary and customise it to your own needs and wants.
Make changes. Scribble in the margins. Cross things out; add
new ones. Spend extra time in one place if it intrigues you, skip

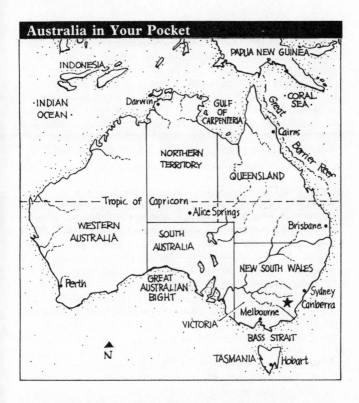

Australia in Your Pocket

another if you find it boring. If there are things you'd like to do in Australia which I haven't listed in this book—by all means, do them.

Each Tour is modular in itself and can be included as part of whatever itinerary you yourself may want to develop. The tours are built with the same sections (though not always in this order):

1. An **Introductory overview** of the tour.
2. A **Suggested schedule** for the tour.
3. A list of **Sightseeing highlights** (rated: ●●●Don't miss; ●●Try hard to see; ●Worthwhile if you can make it).
4. **Orientation,** and an easy-to-read **map** of the area.
5. **Transport** tips and instructions.
6. **Accommodation and eating:** How and where to find the best places in your price range, including addresses, phone numbers and my favourites.
7. **Itinerary options** for those travellers with more or less than the suggested time, or with particular interests.

At the back of the book, I've included some optional tour extensions which expand on the main itinerary. You'll also find sections presenting practical information and cultural insights to add to your appreciation of Australia.

In deciding when and where to launch your trip, consider holiday and event schedules and seasonal weather trends. January to March are the rainiest months along the northern Barrier Reef, for example, while June to September give the Snowy Mountains their name. Spring (October to mid-December) and autumn (mid-March to May) are the best months to cover all corners of this schedule.

Paperwork

To travel to Australia, you will need a valid full passport and a tourist visa. Your tourist visa will cost you nothing except the price of a passport-sized photograph and a self-addressed stamped (and registered) envelope. Your travel agent can handle everything for you. Allow a couple of weeks for processing.

A tourist visa to Australia is typically good for up to six months, with multiple entries allowed for five years or the life of the passport. The tourist visa does prohibit you from working, seeking employment or taking a major course of study while you are in Australia. These require separate visas which must be obtained from outside the country.

Australian consular offices in the UK are located at:

Australian High Commission, Australia House, Strand, London WC2B 4LA (tel. 01-379 4334)

Australian Consulate, Chatsworth House, Lever Street, Manchester M1 2DL (tel. 061-228 1344)

Australian Consulate, 80 Hanover Street, Edinburgh EH2 (tel. 031-226 6271)

Cost considerations

Transport, accommodation, food, etc., are relatively cheap for the tourist. For example, an excellent four-course dinner may be had for A$8 (£3.80), and comfortable hotel rooms may be found for A$30 (£14).

Prices in this book are given in Australian dollars, with an estimated sterling equivalent given in brackets based on an exchange rate of A$2.1 to the pound. These prices are for two people travelling together and sharing hotel rooms. If you are travelling alone, you can expect to spend somewhat more. If you are travelling with a larger group, it will cost you a bit less, especially when it comes to hotel rooms and taxi fares. The cost of public transport and meals won't change much. The cost of

the air fare to and from Australia can range from under £800 to
well over £1,000 depending on the season and the class of ticket.
It is advisable to check with your travel agent for the best deal.
Apart from this cost, budget travellers could just about do this
itinerary for around £400, plus the cost of the Melbourne–Alice
Springs–Cairns–Brisbane legs of the trip. If this is you, you'll
be staying in hostel-style lodging for A$10 (£4.75) a night or less
and travelling by bus or train between Sydney and Melbourne.
You can economise on the internal air fares if it's not important
to keep to a time limit by forking out A$330 (£160) for a 22-day
bus pass, but the additional outlay for extra meals and accommodation will minimise the actual saving.

This trip is ideally suited and designed for the traveller with a
little more money in his or her pocket—say £750 for a three-week
journey, not including getting there and internal flights. If you
are this middle-ground tourist, you'll spend an average of A$25
(£12) a night for a shared hotel room with private facilities, hire a
car for the Sydney–Canberra–Melbourne highway leg, and book
the occasional tour, like a cruise to the outer Barrier Reef.

The traveller who likes to go everywhere in style, to stay at the
best hotels and eat at the best restaurants, will also find this
itinerary appropriate. You can do this within a budget of £1,300
per person, splitting the cost of A$100-a-night (£48) hotel rooms,
hiring a car wherever you want, taking internal flights as
necessary and booking numerous side tours and cruises during
your visit.

The Australian dollar, by the way, is hard to find in paper
these days. It's been replaced in everyday use by a A$1 gold-
coloured coin, leaping kangaroos on the reverse side of the
Queen's portrait. Other coins are the heavy, 12-sided 50-cent
piece, the 20-cent piece, the 10-cent piece, the 5-cent piece, the
2-cent piece, and the 1-cent penny. Paper money, from the lime-
green A$2 note to the blue-grey A$100, grows in size and changes
colour as denominations increase. (In between are $5, $10, $20
and $50 notes.)

It is safest to carry your money in the form of travellers
cheques, which you can exchange at city banks 9:30 a.m. to 4
p.m. Monday to Thursday, 9:30 a.m. to 5 p.m. Friday and at airport currency counters or major hotel desks at any time.

When to go
Australia's big tourist season is during the school holidays which
fall in the middle of summer, appropriately—December, January
and into February. This is the warmest time of year Down
Under, but for four very good reasons this is NOT a time of year
when I would recommend going to Australia:

(1) This is when the Australians are on holiday. You'll find most attractions as well as accommodation heavily booked, and there's a lot of competition to get hold of hire cars, which tends to drive prices up a bit.

(2) This is the rainy season in north Queensland; indeed, it's sometimes the cyclone season. Torrents of rain fall in the northern Barrier Reef (Cairns – Townsville) area, especially from January to March. Don't go without your brolly.

(3) Blowflies—some call them the Australian national bird—are vicious at any time in the Outback, but especially under the hot summer sun.

(4) Perhaps most of all, December to March is classified as 'high season' by international airlines, which jack up their fares during this period.

June, July and August, the British summer but the Australian winter, are superb in the tropics and subtropics, but the further south you go, the less pleasant you're likely to find the weather. Melbourne, for example, can easily have four seasons in a day. What's more, as you travel through Canberra into the Snowy Mountains, you're almost guaranteed to run into snow, and that may cause the closure of some roads.

In my estimation, the ideal times for travel in Australia are autumn (mid-March to May) and spring (September to November). On average, the climate is the best at that time in all parts of the country, and you won't be fighting for rooms like you might be during the peak summer season.

What to bring

As little as possible. Travelling light frees you from the trials of vagabondage to enjoy your journey more thoroughly.

Unless you're in Oz in the winter or are prone to straying into higher elevations, you shouldn't need anything warmer than a sweater and possibly a raincoat. Cairns, in far north Queensland, is at the same latitude south as Jamaica is north, and it's equally as tropical. The southernmost point on the Australian continent, near Melbourne, if flipped across the Equator would be no further north than Malaga in Spain or Rhodes in Greece.

Tend toward lighter clothes, wash-and-wear items that you can wash in your hotel room and dry overnight. I take what I wear and two more sets of everything. Some say I overpack. Australia is a very informal country, and unless you plan to do business on Collins Street in Melbourne (the only city in Australia where a coat and tie are almost a prerequisite), you'll be fine in any situation with a long-sleeved shirt and slacks, or a plain top and wrap-around skirt.

If you're going to use them, bring a camera and lenses (as few as necessary). Buy your film in Australia. You'll want sunglasses for the beaches and the desert; if you get to the Outback and discover you need a wide-brimmed hat with character, choose one there. A good pair of walking shoes is essential. Of course, one thing you should never travel without is a sense of humour.

Getting around in Australia

As I mentioned earlier, within the context of this itinerary, it is most efficient to fly across large chunks of otherwise tedious territory. The most economic way to do this is to check out Ansett Airlines' 'Go Australia' discounted air fares which offer a 20% discount on the ordinary economy fare provided the total distance flown on each leg is over 1,000 km. Tickets can be purchased in the UK before departure through your travel agent who will be able to provide further details.

Ansett is one of two major domestic carriers in Australia. The other, Australian Airlines, is every bit as good. For our purposes, though, there's one significant difference: Ansett has the sole concession on Alice Springs to Ayers Rock air travel. Australian Airlines has a routing edge only in flights to outback Queensland.

Two other transport pass options may interest budget travellers—bus and train. Three separate coach firms with extensive national routes offer passes for unlimited travel within their city-to-city express systems. Deluxe Coachlines, the 'Avis' ('we try harder') of the three, has a 'Koalapass' valid for 10 to 90 days. (A 15-day pass is A$240 (£115), a 22-day pass A$330 (£160), a 62-day pass A$670 (£320).) Greyhound has passes for 14 (A$250 (£120)) to 60 ($690 (£330)) days, while Ansett Pioneer's 'Aussiepass' is valid for 15 (A$260 (£125)) to 60 (A$690 (£330)) days. Ansett advertises free city sightseeing in some cities, discount tours in others, for passholders. Discount motel packages are also available in concert with the coach passes.

Railways of Australia have an 'Austrailpass' valid for unlimited first-class travel, and a 'Budget Austrailpass' for unlimited economy travel, on its route system. (This system is limited: the only way to travel from Alice Springs to Cairns is via Sydney.) The minimum duration is 14 days (A$440 (£210) first-class, A$290 (£140) budget); one month is A$450 (£215) budget, three months cost A$730 (£350) budget. There's an additional charge for overnight berths (A$20 (£9.50) Brisbane – Cairns, for example; A$33 (£16) Adelaide – Alice Springs; A$99 (£48) Melbourne – Perth).

My major objection to travel by train or bus is that they carry you only from urban area to urban area. You don't see rural Australia except through smoked windows. Buses and trains pass through an area only two or three times daily; if you want to

disembark and take a closer look at something interesting, you're
going to have a long wait before the next coach passes through.
You wouldn't even get to the exquisite Victorian gold town of
Beechworth; the main-line buses don't go there. And how could
you possibly do a wine-tasting tour of Australia's great vineyard
districts by bus or train?

Hiring a car and driving

The best way to see southeastern Australia is to drive your own
vehicle. A car allows you much more freedom in your travels,
plus an opportunity to get in touch with the 'real' Australia. Part
of this itinerary is geared for the car traveller. If two of you, or
better yet, four are travelling together, you'll share the costs of
the vehicle and really cut your expenses.

To hire a car in Australia, you must be over 21 years old,
preferably have a major credit card, and definitely have a valid
driver's licence. It is also necessary for you to have an
international driver's licence.

All major airports have a handful of hire-car agencies: many are
also located in central city areas near major hotels. In Sydney,
check the agencies on William Street between the city centre and
King's Cross. While Hertz and Avis are the old standbys, you'll
probably get a better rate from Thrifty or from any number of
smaller, locally owned firms.

Plan on an outlay of A$45 to A$55 a day (about £20 to £25),
including limited kilometres. Petrol, in New South Wales and
Victoria priced at 50 to 55 Australian cents a litre (about £1.10 to
£1.20 a gallon) will be your only other major driving expense.
(The cost of petrol is slightly cheaper in South Australia and
southeastern Queensland, a bit higher in Tasmania and Western
Australia.)

Remember that Australia, like most nations of the world,
employs the metric system of measurement. There are roughly
4½ litres to one UK gallon. Eight kilometres equal about five
miles.

In the cities you don't need a car, and shouldn't use one. It's
not worth the frustration, between rush-hour traffic, parking
hassles and confusing local laws. (Central Melbourne, for
instance, requires drivers to pull all the way to the left of an
intersection and wait for traffic to clear before turning *right*.)
Inner city public transport is very good. Buses, Sydney subways
and Melbourne trams are all excellent. Taxis are moderately
priced. Turn your car in on arrival in a new city and save
yourself many headaches.

The only roads in Australia that are really in good condition are
the main highways—particularly the Sydney to Melbourne Hume

Highway, a four-lane thoroughfare. Many other roads are in less than optimum shape, tarmacked but with no shoulders and with lots of ruts and potholes.

Those signs warning of 'Next 10 km' of kangaroos or other Aussie animals should be more than curiosities, especially to night drivers. You won't often see wild animals in the daytime, but please drive carefully after dark.

Where to stay

Australia has a real choice here, with accommodation of all standards at all price levels.

I rate budget accommodation as that costing A$15 (£7) and less a night; economy A$15 to A$40 (£7 to £20), moderate A$40 to A$80 (£20 to £40) and deluxe over A$80 (£40). There are a number of categories to consider.

Hotels run the full gamut from the internationally ranked Regent of Sydney all the way down to the corner pub with a few basic rooms in the attic. Deluxe to economy.

Private hotels are not licensed to sell alcohol, and therefore are usually lower in cost. Moderate and economy.

Guest houses are private hotels that provide bed and breakfast, often (but not always) included in the tariff. Moderate and economy.

Self-catering apartments are, in essence, hotel suites with their own cooking facilities, and sometimes private laundry facilities. Deluxe and moderate.

Motels in Australia offer much the same as their British counterparts. Deluxe to economy.

Hostels may or may not be members of the International Youth Hostel Federation. IYH member hostels are located in cities, towns and national parks throughout the country. Private 'backpackers' hostels' with similar price structures are more recent developments in major cities and tourist centres. Budget.

Caravan parks are not only for caravans. You can set up a tent or, in many cases, stay in a small self-catering cabin with a hotplate. Budget.

Farm holidays will place you on a 'station' far from the bright city lights, where you can watch the dogs muster the sheep—or help a jackeroo round up his cattle by helicopter. Write: 9 Fletcher St., Woollahra, Sydney, NSW 2025, for details. Moderate and economy.

What and where to eat and drink

Australia is a very cosmopolitan country. This is especially true in Sydney and Melbourne, which have very large populations of south Europeans, Lebanese and Asians. Nowhere is their influence felt more strongly than in the variety and quality of reasonably priced cuisine. You can eat well at any meal for under A$10 (£4.75). If you plan to spend A$20 (£9.50) per day per person on food, you're perhaps being a little bit extravagant—or else you're budgeting for an occasional slap up at a classier restaurant.

Though not widely acknowledged, there *is* an Australian cuisine somewhat more imaginative than the bland British and Irish cooking from which it is derived. Aussie 'tucker' comprises occasionally palatable dishes such as kangaroo tail soup, meat pies, 'snags' (large sausages), damper (unleavened campfire bread) and Vegemite (a strong-tasting yeast spread); and more delectable delicacies like carpetbagger steak (tenderloin stuffed with Sydney rock oysters), roast lamb in mint sauce, pavlova (a meringue dessert), and superb seafood—yabbies (a small lobster), Moreton Bay bugs (another small crustacean), Tasmanian scallops, and indigenous fish like barramundi, jewfish and John Dory.

I will typically begin my day in Australia with a light breakfast of fresh fruit—pawpaws (papayas) and mangoes are always in season—and/or pastry with a cup of tea or coffee. Later in the morning I might stop for Devonshire tea, served with fresh scones (with whipped cream and strawberry jam).

For lunch, I might pick up some fish and chips or a chicko roll at the takeaway counter of a milk bar (sort of corner grocery with a fast food counter). More often, I'll pause for pub grub. You never really go wrong if you go to eat in a pub. The price is right—often A$4 to A$6 (£1.90 to £2.85) for a full meal—and you can pick some pretty good meals off the blackboard menu: roast chicken, grilled fish, steak-and-kidney pie, even cook your own T-bone.

At dinnertime, I'll often head off to the European or Asian section of town, read the menus posted in the windows and wander in where I see the locals eating. And I almost always wash it down with a glass of good Aussie beer or wine. Many restaurants acclaim themselves as 'BYO': bring your own alcohol. They may charge a small corkage fee, but their prices are almost always lower than licensed restaurants, and it's no great inconvenience to stop by the off-licence at a nearby pub.

Beer is the Australian national drink, and it certainly deserves that distinction. Those who compile such statistics say the Aussies drink more beer per capita—some 30 gallons annually—than anyone but the Bavarians and Belgians. Every state has its own breweries and is stubbornly proud of its local brews. Drink from 'middies' or 'pots' or from 'schooners'.

Australian wine has become recognised as among the best in the world. The principal growing areas are the Barossa Valley, focused on Tanunda northeast of Adelaide, and the Hunter Valley, around Cessnock north of Sydney. Victoria and Western Australian also have excellent wineries. Riesling, semillon, chardonnay and white burgundy are among the better white wines; in the reds, consider claret, cabernet sauvignon, shiraz and merlot.

Information sources

This slender tome is not intended to be more than a travel planner to be used in conjunction with a more complete guidebook.

Lonely Planet's *Australia: A Travel Survival Kit,* by Tony Wheeler et al., has long been the bible of shoestring travellers in Australia, and deservedly so. The book has grown to become a very comprehensive volume of some 400 pages thoroughly covering the entire continent. It is a book that no traveller, especially no budget traveller, should go without. An option, not as detailed nationwide but reasonably good in the major cities, is Frommer's *Australia on $25 a Day* by John Godwin. For middle and upper-income travellers looking to get the most quality for their money, I highly recommend Robert W. Bone's *Maverick Guide to Australia* (Pelican, available through Horizon Books). An excellent book for planning your trip, and as a souvenir when your trip is over, is Apa Productions' lavishly illustrated *Insight Guide: Australia.* You should be able to find all of these books at good quality bookshops in the UK. Other useful guides include the *Australia* volume in the well-known Michelin Guide series, and *The Australia Travellers' Guide* published by and available from the Australian Tourist Commission.

In planning, don't overlook the assistance you can get from the Australian Tourist Commission and from the individual state and territory tourist boards. They can provide an enormous amount of valuable information for your journey. They also can provide the best highway maps I've found on Australia and its separate states.

Australian Tourist Commission
  4th Floor, Heathcote House, 20 Savile Row, London W1X 1AE (tel. 01-434 4372)
New South Wales Tourism Commission
  New South Wales House, 66 Strand, London WC2N 5LZ (tel. 01-839 6651)
Northern Territory Tourism Commission
  4th Floor, 393 Strand, London WC2R 0LZ (tel. 01-836 3344)
Queensland Tourist and Travel Corporation
  Queensland House, 392 Strand, London WC2R 0LZ (tel. 01-836 1333)

Agent General for South Australia
  South Australia House, 50 Strand, London WC2N 5LW (tel.
01-930 7471)
Tasmania
  (See under Australian Tourist Commission above.)
Agent General for Victoria
  Victoria House, Melbourne Place, Strand, London WC2B 4LG
(tel. 01-836 2656)
Western Australia Tourism Commission
  Western Australia House, 115 Strand, London WC2R 0AJ (tel.
01-240 2881)

Other reading

Nearly all Aussies identify with the Outback, the 'bush', even if
they are (as most are) urban dwellers. To get a feeling for this
tradition, I would go back to the short stories and poetry of 19th
century writers Henry Lawson and A.B. 'Banjo' Paterson. Lawson
is more highly acclaimed in Australia, though Paterson's
ballads—'Waltzing Matilda', 'The Man from Snowy River' — are
better known.

  The best Australian novel in recent years is Colleen
McCullough's *The Thorn Birds*. Some people may know the mini-
series (starring Richard Chamberlain) better than the book. A
young Aussie writer who impresses me is Tim Winton (*That Eye,
the Sky*).

  Good histories are Donald Horne's *The Australian People:
Biography of a Nation* and F.R. Crowley's *A New History of
Australia*. Robert Hughes' superb *The Fatal Shore* (1987) deals
with Australia's convict history and, indirectly, its impact on the
modern nation. For a better understanding of Aboriginal history
and culture, see *Australian Dreaming* edited by Jennifer Isaacs.
Titles by Michael Morcombe and Eric Worrell are among the
best dealing with Australia's rich natural history.

ITINERARY

Most people have only, if they're lucky, three weeks of holiday in which to see Australia. So here is my suggested itinerary, which I hope provides the best sampling of the country in a limited period of time. I encourage you to add days for relaxation whenever possible, because the pace of travel—over 4,000 miles in a very short time—can be exhausting.

Here is an overview of the itinerary:

TOUR 1 Arrive in Sydney in the morning, get settled in your accommodation, then enjoy an afternoon cruise on beautiful Sydney Harbour. Call it quits right after dinner tonight, cheating jet lag with an early bedtime.

TOUR 2 The Sydney Explorer bus will escort you to all major city sights for one set fare. Highlights will include the famous Opera House; the Australian Museum; and The Rocks, Sydney's oldest neighbourhood. Enjoy an atmospheric dinner at the Argyle Tavern in The Rocks, with bush ballad sing-alongs.

TOUR 3 Exercise your options. I like to start the day at Bondi Beach, then visit the colonial Vaucluse House mansion and wander through the suburbs of Double Day and Paddington. If it's marsupials you want to see, take the ferry across the harbour to Taronga Park Zoo, and include a visit to Manly, with its famous surf beach and Marineland. History buffs may want to visit Old Sydney Town in Gosford; oenophiles (wine buffs!) should make a side trip to the Hunter Valley. Spend the night at Kings Cross, where you can play or gawp at others playing.

TOUR 4 Pick up your reserved hire car in Sydney early this morning, with plans to leave it in Melbourne in a week. After a stop to see the working sheep farm at Gledswood homestead, continue to historic Berrima for lunch. On arrival in Canberra, visit the Regatta Point Planning Exhibition to understand the design and evolution of this modern capital, then drive to the top of Mount Ainslie for a good overview.

TOUR 5 Explore Canberra. Start at the Parliament House, if possible watching the House of Representatives or Senate in session from a public gallery. Take a drive through the Yarralumla area to see the impressive row of national embassies, then lunch at the High Court, inspect the National Gallery and visit the Australian War Memorial museum.

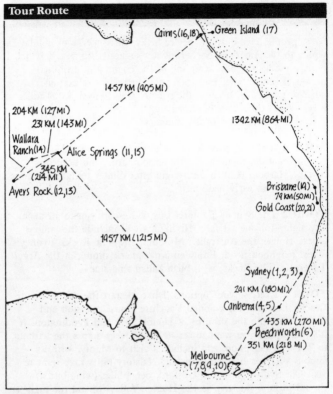

Tour Route

Cairns (16,18) • Green Island (17)

1457 KM (905 MI)

204 KM (127 MI)
231 KM (143 MI)

Wallara
Ranch (14)   Alice Springs (11,15)

345 KM
(214 MI)

Ayers Rock (12,13)

1392 KM (864 MI)

Brisbane (19)
74 KM (50 MI)
Gold Coast (20,21)

1957 KM (1215 MI)

Sydney (1,2,3)
291 KM (180 MI)
Canberra (4,5)
435 KM (270 MI)
Beechworth (6)
351 KM (218 MI)
Melbourne
(7,8,9,10)

TOUR 6 There's a long day of driving ahead, so get an early start. Today's route leads past the alpine resort of Thredbo in the Snowy Mountains, and via Corryong, reputed home of poet Banjo Paterson's 'Man from Snowy River', to Beechworth, a town straight out of the 19th century gold-rush era.

TOUR 7 After a morning look at Beechworth, visit the Brown Brothers Winery, one of Australia's finest, and stop in Glenrowan, where Ned Kelly, Australia's most notorious 19th century bushranger, made his 'last stand'. The afternoon's highlight is the Sir Colin McKenzie Wildlife Sanctuary at Healesville, an open-air reserve that is the best of its kind in the world. You'll reach Melbourne in time for dinner.

TOUR 8 Explore Melbourne today. Wander through its ethnic neighbourhoods, its sophisticated shopping arcades, its highbrow business district. Don't miss the beautiful Victorian Arts Centre or the nation's best botanic gardens. The Old Gaol and the National Museum are worthwhile stops. But don't overdo the sightseeing. Here in sports-crazy Melbourne, you should soak up some Australian culture with (depending on the season) a visit to a 'footie' match, a cricket test or a horse race.

TOUR 9 Drive to Ballarat, site of Australia's greatest gold rush and its most famous rebellion. The Sovereign Hill theme park realistically recreates the town's heyday. The adjacent Gold Museum and the Eureka Exhibition memorialise Eureka Stockade. Return to Melbourne in the late afternoon.

TOUR 10 Drive east into the Dandenong Ranges, where you can wonder at William Ricketts' unique forest sculptures, search for lyrebirds in Sherbrooke Forest, or take a ride on the Puffing Billy. Proceed to Phillip Island, where fairy penguins parade from the sea at dusk. Then return to Melbourne.

TOUR 11 Drop your car at Melbourne's Tullamarine airport and catch a morning flight to Alice Springs. You'll have all afternoon and evening to explore this Outback oasis. Stop by the Old Telegraph Station, the Royal Flying Doctor Service and the Aboriginal art galleries. Climax your day with something unique: ride a camel down the dry Todd River bed to dinner at a desert winery.

TOUR 12 Marvel at the weird geology of the Red Centre as you fly from Alice Springs to Yulara resort village at Ayers Rock, arriving in the early afternoon. After getting settled in your lodging and exploring the community, join the sunset barbecue tour to The Olgas.

TOUR 13 Learn about the Aboriginal culture today. Spend the morning with a native guide who will show you how his people found food, water, shelter and medicine in this arid landscape. Visit the craft exhibit at the Uluru National Park ranger station and search for ancient petroglyphs in caves around the base of Ayers Rock. Back at Yulara, sip champagne as you watch the sun set over the red rock. Turn in early, because tomorrow, if you're energetic, you will . . .

TOUR 14 . . . climb The Rock. If the world's largest monolith is awesome at sunset, it's even more stunning at dawn. Wake early to watch the light change its appearance, and to beat the heat and flies as you scale the huge red rock so that you, too, can wear a T-shirt declaring: 'I Climbed Ayers Rock'. Then board a bus for the 125-mile drive to the Wallara Ranch, where you'll spend the night at an Outback station.

TOUR 15 Scramble through the sheer walls of colourful Kings Canyon, then return to Alice Springs in the evening. If you're not exhausted, enjoy a nightcap at the casino.

TOUR 16 A travel day, Alice Springs to Cairns. On arrival in Cairns, the humidity will tell you immediately that you are in the tropics. Have a cold beer at an Esplanade pub and watch the fishing and pleasure boats come and go to the Great Barrier Reef. For dinner, order barramundi, a delectable river-run reef cod.

TOUR 17 Take a boat to Green Island, a tiny coral enclave 40 minutes' cruise offshore where you can swim, study the sea life from a glass-bottom boat, view the largest crocodile in captivity in the world, and dine, drink and sleep at the small resort.

TOUR 18 You'll leave Green Island this morning to spend the day snorkelling or diving on the outer Barrier Reef. This experience should not be missed. More than 200 species of tropical reef fish can be seen swimming through a fantastic undersea 'garden' of multicoloured coral. Return to Cairns at night.

TOUR 19 The scenic Kuranda Railway will take you inland to the edge of the rainforested Atherton Tableland, climbing steeply above fields of sugar cane to the Barron River Gorge. In Kuranda, you'll have time to see Barron Falls, the open-air market and the Noctarium before returning to Cairns after lunch. Take a late afternoon flight to Brisbane.

TOUR 20 Brisbane's No. 1 tourist sight is the Lone Pine Koala Sanctuary, Australia's largest. If you ever wanted a photo of yourself holding one of these seemingly cuddly creatures, here's where to have it taken. Travel there by boat up the Brisbane River. After lunch, take a bus to the Gold Coast. Catch the day's last rays on the beach.

TOUR 21 Your final day on Australian beaches. The Gold Coast's biggest town is called Surfers Paradise; why not decide for yourself if the name really fits? Or you can dive into tourist attractions like Sea World, the Currumbin Bird Sanctuary or the Mudgeeraba Boomerang Factory.

TOUR 22 Fly Home from Brisbane.

TOUR 1

ARRIVE IN SYDNEY

Welcome to Australia! This is your first day Down Under, but
you have many more to come, so don't exhaust yourself too
quickly. After clearing customs and immigration, travel into the
city, get settled in your hotel, refresh yourself, then spend the
afternoon on a leisurely cruise of the beautiful Sydney Harbour.

Suggested schedule

Morning	Arrive at Sydney Airport and take a bus into the city. Get set up in your accommodation and have lunch.
2:00 p.m.	Sydney Harbour 'Coffee Cruise' from Circular Quay. Or take a ferry to Manly.
5:00 p.m.	Return to hotel.
6:30 p.m.	Dinner in Darlinghurst.
9:00 p.m.	Collapse into bed.

Airport orientation

Kingsford Smith (Sydney) International Airport is located about
10 km south of the city centre on Botany Bay. (Start thinking in
metrics as soon as you arrive: 10 kilometres is about six miles.)
When your plane drops in over the bay, you'll be arriving Down
Under at almost the exact place as did Captain James Cook, the
first European to visit Australia, in 1770. Unlike Cook, you'll
have to clear immigration and customs. Cap'n Jim was fortunate
not to have to go through those formalities two centuries ago.

Travellers unlucky enough to arrive at the same time as a half-
dozen other international flights will disagree, but I've always
found the immigration procedures relatively painless here.
Hopefully, you'll zoom through quite quickly, wait a few
minutes to pluck your luggage from the baggage carousels, then
move straight through customs into the arrival hall.

Change some money into Australian dollars at the airport bank,
to the right. The rate here isn't quite as good as you'll find at the
banks in the city, but the hotel counters are open to meet all
incoming international flights and if you've followed my
suggestion and arrived on a Saturday, you'll need enough cash to
get you through the weekend. (Incidentally, some banks charge as
much as A$5 (£2.40) commission for transactions; others none.
Inquire before you exchange.)

At the south end of the arrival hall (furthest from the bank) is the Travellers Information Service desk. Here you can obtain hotel reservations, maps, information on tourist attractions in Sydney, and book a shuttle bus ticket into town. A bus ticket, which entitles you to be dropped off at most hotels within the City Centre – Kings Cross area, costs A\$3 (£1.40). Taxis cost about A\$10 (£4.75). Turn a cold shoulder on the hire car agents for now: you don't need one in the city. Public transport is excellent, and you'll save a lot of money, not to mention parking and driving hassles, if you wait to pick up a car until you leave Sydney in three days.

If you haven't yet booked your domestic flight segments, take the escalator upstairs to the departure hall and do it now. If you're wielding a 'Go Australian Airpass', you'll need Ansett Flight 77 from Melbourne to Alice Springs at 10 a.m. on Tour 11; Ansett NT Flight BT278 from Alice Springs to Ayers Rock at 11:35 a.m. on Tour 12; Ansett Flight 285 from Alice Springs to Cairns at 10:55 a.m. on Tour 16; and Ansett Flight 39 from Cairns to Brisbane at 5:15 p.m. on Tour 19.

Sydney orientation

Over 20% of all Australians live in metropolitan Sydney. These 3½ million lucky people make their homes in one of the great cities on earth. It has everything they might ask: a beautiful setting around a long, deep-blue harbour, a rich and varied cultural life, restaurants and hotels to suit all tastes and spending abilities, and activities enough to fill this whole book.

Not only is Sydney Australia's largest city, it was also its first. On 26 January 1788, Captain Arthur Phillip arrived in Port Jackson (Sydney Harbour) with his 'First Fleet' of 11 ships. He landed close to the site of the modern Harbour Bridge and established a settlement in the area known today as The Rocks. Nearly three-quarters of his 1,030 passengers were convicts, most of them deported from the British Isles for petty thievery, forgery and similar charges. They became the foundation of the colony and the nation, and it is their success that Australia celebrated in its Bicentennial observance in 1988.

The oldest buildings standing in Sydney today are a legacy of Governor Lachlan Macquarie (1809 – 1821), who set an egalitarian standard for Australia by ordering the emancipation of deserving convicts to give them a 'fair go' alongside free settlers. Yet it wasn't until the 20th century, first with Commonwealth status ('independence') in 1901 and later with an influx of European immigrants, that the city really boomed.

Sydney's climate is similar to that of Los Angeles in the USA—without the smog. The mean summer temperature

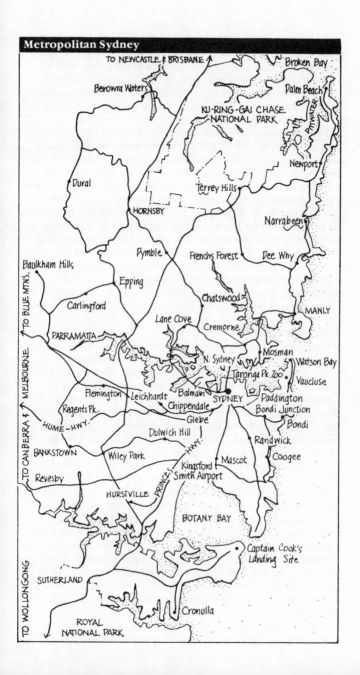

Metropolitan Sydney

(December to February) is 78 degrees Fahrenheit; the winter
mean (June to August) is 55 degrees. Average annual rainfall is
47.5 inches, with June the rainiest month (5.1 inches) and
September the driest (0.6 inches). With such a comfortable
climate, Sydneysiders love the outdoors. On most weekends and
sunny afternoons you'll find them on their boats in the harbour
or on the many fine beaches.

Though Sydney sprawls for many miles around the harbour, it's
easy to find your way around the central area. Circular Quay,
where ferries and cruise boats dock, is your point of orientation.
East of the Quay, jutting into the harbour on Bennelong Point, is
the Opera House, and immediately south of it the botanic gardens
and The Domain. Macquarie Street is the main north–south
thoroughfare here. West of the Quay, George and Pitt Streets run
from The Rocks (at the foot of the Harbour Bridge) through the
City Centre to Chinatown and the central railway station. Park
Street (becoming William Street) intersects George and Pitt
Streets at Sydney Town Hall and proceeds east, dissecting Hyde
Park and running about a mile to Kings Cross. The Martin Place
pedestrian precinct, halfway between Park Street and Circular
Quay, spans five streets from George Street to Macquarie Street.

City transport

Between the subway/train, the bus and the ferry system, Sydney
is extremely well served by all forms of public transport.

The Sydney Metropolitan Rail System (tel. 20942) served 176
stations in nine lines running west, south, north and east of
Central Station. The City Circle subway line runs continuously
from 4:30 a.m. to midnight between Museum, St James, Circular
Quay, Wynyard, Town Hall and Central stations; the Eastern
Suburbs line connects Town Hall with Martin Place, Kings Cross
and on to Bondi Junction. System-wide maps can be obtained
from any visitor information centre. Standard fares for short
distances are 60 cents (28p).

Buses of the Urban Transit Authority of New South Wales (tel.
20543) serve every corner of the metropolis that the trains miss.
Fares start at 60 cents (28p). A free bus service (No. 777)
operates in the central city area at 10-minute intervals from 9:30
a.m. to 3:30 p.m. Monday to Friday. Another free bus (No. 666)
connects Wynyard station with the Art Gallery of New South
Wales in The Domain. Tourists are well served by the Sydney
Explorer, a bright red double-decker bus which runs an 18-km
loop to 20 major attractions for a set fee of A$7.50 (£3.50). The
service operates continuously from 9:30 a.m. to 5 p.m. daily at
15-minute intervals.

The Urban Transit Authority also operates the ferry service

from Circular Quay (tel. 219-4735) between 6 a.m. and 11 p.m. daily. The one-way fare is A$1 (48p) west to Hunters Hill and Greenwich, or across the harbour to Mosman, Cremorne and Neutral Bay. To Manly, near the head of the harbour, it costs A$1.30 (60p) by ferry or A$2.40 (£1.15) by hydrofoil.

Two special fares allow travellers to take advantage of all transport systems for a reduced cost. The Day Rover, priced at A$3.80 (£1.80), is good for unlimited travel on train, ferry (but not hydrofoil) and bus (except the Sydney Explorer) within the Sydney area weekdays after 9 a.m., or at any time weekends. The Weekly Rover, good for seven consecutive days under similar conditions, costs A$19 (£9).

Where to stay

Sydney's best hotels are a boomerang's throw from Circular Quay and The Rocks. The **Regent of Sydney,** 199 George Street (tel. 238-0000) is ranked among the world's elite: it's very expensive... but worth every penny, I'm told. Just down the street, and a small step down in price, is the **Old Sydney Parkroyal,** right in The Rocks at 55 George Street (tel. 20524).

For lower cost lodging, the best selection is in Kings Cross, Sydney's answer to London's Soho and Paris' Pigalle. There's a lot of bustle and sleaze (some call it 'character') here, but no real danger as long as you mind your own business. In the moderate price bracket, check out the **Merlin Plaza,** a self-catering apartment hotel at 2 Springfield Avenue (tel. 356-3255). For an economy class bed, the nearby **Springfield Lodge,** 9 Springfield Avenue (tel. 358-3222), has old-world charm.

For real budget accommodation, look on Victoria Street and Hughes Street, where you'll pay as little as A$6 (£2.80) a night in a dormitory (perhaps A$15 (£7.20) a night in a shared double room) at a dozen small private hotels and backpackers' hostels. There's not a lot to choose between these places; I opt for the places with TV and rec rooms, not to mention good travellers' bulletin boards. Try **The Traveller's Rest,** 156 Victoria Street (tel. 358-4606), or **The Downunder Hostel,** 25 Hughes Street (tel. 358-1143). No hostel in the Cross is a member of the International Youth Hostel Federation; there are IYH hostels further out at 262 Glebe Point Road, Glebe (tel. 692-8418); 28 Ross Street, Forest Lodge (tel. 692-0747), near Sydney University; and 407 Marrickville Road, Dulwich Hill (tel. 569-0272).

Where to eat

The best restaurant strip in Sydney, both in terms of price and variety of cuisine, is Oxford Street in Darlinghurst, less than 1 km south of Kings Cross via Darlinghurst Road or Victoria

Street. For less than A\$10 (£5) per person, you can eat well at
such diverse ethnic eateries as **Raquel's Ole Madrid** (Spanish,
No. 145), **La Bella Notte** (Italian, No. 201), the **Balkan** (Greek,
No. 209–215), **Momotaro** (Japanese, No. 225), **Kim** (No. 235,
Vietnamese) or **Borobudur** (Indonesian, No. 263), among many
others. Around the corner and down the street are Sydney's best
selections for budget-watchers—**No Name** (that's what locals call
it; it really doesn't have a name), 2 Chapel Street, a half-block
south of Stanley Street off Crown Street, and the **Metro Cafe,**
26 Burton Street west of Crown. At either, you can get simple
but huge pasta-and-salad meals for around A\$5 (£2.40). Two
doors down from the Metro on Burton is the **Different
Drummer,** a licensed establishment (the others are all BYO) in a
lovely garden setting where steak or seafood dinners cost A\$6 to
A\$7 (£2.80 to £3.30). **Laurie's,** opposite Green Park at Victoria
and Burton Streets, has innovative vegetarian cuisine.

In the Cross, you'll get a square meal for a fair price at the
Bayswater Brasserie, 32 Bayswater Road. Other moderate-
priced options: **Majit's Renamed Amar's,** 69 Macleay Street,
for Indian curries, and **Benny's,** 12–14 Challis Avenue, for
Japanese and Malay cuisine.

In the centre you can dine like an affluent tourist at the
Bennelong Restaurant in the Opera House, or in higher style
yet in the revolving restaurants atop **Sydney Tower** or
Australia Square (which is round, incidentally). More popular
among locals in a moderate price range are **Johnny Walker's
Bistro** in Angel Place (near Martin Place) for steaks; the
Sorrento, 5 Elizabeth Street (basement), for seafood; **The Old
Spaghetti Factory,** 80 George Street, The Rocks, for pasta and
atmosphere; **Pancakes on the Rocks,** 10 Hickson Road, for
24-hour munchies; and the **Imperial Peking Harbourside,** 15
Circular Quay West, for upmarket Chinese food.

If you want to eat like the Asians, though, visit the **Chinatown
Food Fair,** Dixon and Goulburn Streets (third floor). Open from
11 a.m. to 11 p.m. daily (to 9 p.m. Sundays), you can sate your
appetite for under A\$5 (£2.50) while choosing your meal from
over a dozen Southeast Asia-style food stalls. There's a smaller
version of the same at **Dixon Gourmet,** Dixon and Little Hay
Streets.

Away from Sydney's core, two restaurants deserve a special
mention. **Doyle's on the Beach,** at Watson's Bay near the south
head of the harbour mouth, is so famous for its seafood that it
runs a special shuttle ferry from a dock near Circular Quay. The
Berowra Waters Inn, Berowra, is considered the best of all
possible restaurants in Australia. To get there, you must drive an
hour north from the city centre to a jetty, where you are met by

a private punt. It's open Friday to Sunday only, and bookings are required.

Helpful hints

The **Sydney Visitors Bureau** (tel. 235-2424) is in Martin Place at Elizabeth Street, smack in the middle of the centre. The office provides maps and brochures, and books seats for tours or entertainment events, 9 a.m. to 5 p.m. weekdays.

The **General Post Office** is also on Martin Place at the corner of Pitt Street. Banks are open 9:30 a.m. to 4 p.m. Monday to Thursday, 9:30 a.m. to 5 p.m. Friday. Most shops are open from 9 a.m. to 5:30 p.m. Monday to Wednesday, 9 a.m. to 9 p.m. Thursday and Friday, 9 a.m. to 12 noon Saturday.

In case of emergencies, dial 000.

TOUR 2

AROUND SYDNEY

Today is devoted to exploring the major sights of the city's core.
Take the red double-decker bus, the Sydney Explorer (see 'City
Transport', Tour 1), or—better yet—walk.

Suggested schedule

8:00 a.m.	Breakfast at hotel.
9:00 a.m.	Take the bus, subway or walk to the Opera House, arriving for the guided tour.
10:30 a.m.	Experience the view from Sydney Tower.
11:15 a.m.	Browse through Hyde Park Barracks and The Old Mint.
12:30 p.m.	Picnic lunch in The Domain or Botanic Gardens.
1:30 p.m.	Art Gallery of NSW.
3:00 p.m.	Australian Museum.
4:30 p.m.	The Rocks: Start a walking tour at the visitor centre, but dawdle in the shops and pubs.
7:30 p.m.	Dinner and show at the Argyle Tavern.

Sightseeing highlights

● ● ● **Sydney Harbour** (see Tour 1)—Life in Sydney centres
on the Harbour. Thirteen miles (21 km) long from its ocean
heads to the mouth of the Paramatta River, with some 160 miles
(250 km) of crenellated coastline, the deep blue inlet seems
permanently speckled with boats of all sizes and shapes. On
sunny weekend afternoons, the colourful jibs of myriad sailboats
make the harbour look like a seaborne carnival. The Opera House
and Harbour Bridge are its unmistakable landmarks, but there is
much more to see: colonial mansions and modern architectural
showcases, the skylines of central and North Sydney, the laughing
face and looming roller coaster of Luna Park, the sandstone
turrets of Fort Denison on venerable Pinchgut Island.

All Harbour cruises leave the city from Circular Quay, at the
foot of Pitt Street. Ferry routes and fares are discussed in Tour 1
under 'City Transport'. There's also a Sydney Harbour Explorer:
for a flat fee of A$12 (£5.75), you can spend the day shuttling
between the Opera House, The Rocks, Pier 1, the Taronga Park
Zoo and Watson Bay. The Explorer leaves Circular Quay daily at
10:25 and 11:55 a.m., 1:25 and 2:55 p.m. Ninety minute

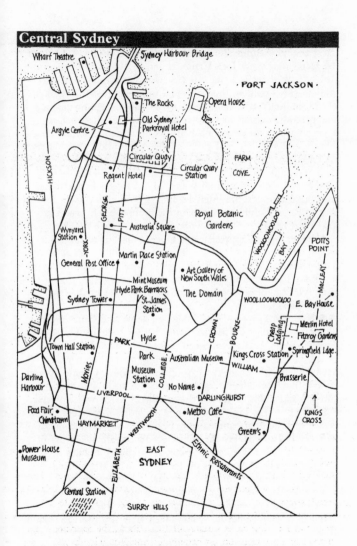

Central Sydney

stopovers are permitted, with free reboarding.

There are several cruise operators. I like Captain Cook Cruises, with 14 tour options daily from 9 a.m. to 7:30 p.m., varying in length from 75 minutes to six hours and in price from $9 to $41.50 (£4.30 to £19.75). A good introductory trip is the Captain Cook Coffee Cruise, leaving Pier 6 every day at 10 a.m. and 2 p.m. The 2½ hour trip includes refreshments.

● ● ● **Sydney Opera House,** Bennelong Point. One of the
most unique buildings on earth, the Opera House was designed
by Danish architect Jorn Utzon, begun in 1959 and opened in
1973. Talk about inflation: its cost was first estimated at A$7
million (£3.3 million), but it wound up costing A$102 million
(£48.6 million)! It's really much more than a stage for operas; the
complex also contains a concert hall, a theatre, a cinema, a
recording hall, an exhibition hall, two restaurants, six lounges, a
library and archives, and various rehearsal studios, dressing rooms
and administrative offices, all under the distinctive sail-like roofs.

Sixty-minute guided tours are conducted daily (except Good
Friday and Christmas) from 9 a.m. to 4 p.m. Backstage tours,
lasting 90 minutes, are offered Sundays only. They start from the
Music Room-Exhibition foyer on the ground level; tickets are
A$3.50 (£1.65).

A better way to appreciate the Opera House is to take in a
performance. You can get a full schedule of all events at most
visitor centres. The Opera House box office is open Monday to
Saturday from 9 a.m. to 8:30 p.m., and Sunday from 9 a.m. to 4
p.m. You can also book by phone (with a major credit card) by
calling 20525.

● ● **Sydney Tower**—Rises 1,000 feet above the Centrepoint
shopping complex off Market Street between Pitt and Castlereagh
Streets. Some Aussie cynics call this edifice 'the bucket on the
stick', but as the highest public building in the Southern
Hemisphere, it's worth the trip up for the view. Open 9:30 a.m.
to 9:30 p.m. Monday to Saturday, 10:30 a.m. to 4:30 p.m.
Sunday and public holidays; closed Christmas. It will cost you
A$3.50 (£1.65) to take the lift up. Lunch and dinner are served in
a pair of restaurants immediately below the observation deck.

● ● **Hyde Park Barracks**—On Queen's Square at the top of
Macquarie Street. Designed by convict architect Francis
Greenway (whose picture is on the A$10 note) and erected in
1819 as a dormitory for male convicts, it has become an
interesting museum of Sydney social history. Start on the top
floor to learn in considerable detail about the shipment of
convicts from England to Sydney, then step down to the second
floor to trace the city's 19th century development. Open 10 a.m.
to 5 p.m. daily (noon to 5 p.m. Tuesday); closed Good Friday
and Christmas. Free admission.

● **The Old Mint**—Next door to the Barracks. One of Australia's
oldest public buildings (1817), it was built as a hospital wing but
became the first branch of the British Royal Mint outside
London after gold was discovered in 1851. Since 1982, it has
been an elegant, well-organised museum of decorative art, coins
and stamps. Open 10 a.m. to 5 p.m. daily (noon to 5 p.m.

Wednesday); closed Good Friday and Christmas. Free admission.
● **Art Gallery of New South Wales**--Art Gallery Road, The
Domain. Sydney's (but not Australia's) best art museum, it is
interesting for its survey of Aussie paintings through the 19th and
20th centuries. A major 1987–88 expansion has added a
sculpture terrace, Asian art gallery and several theatres. Open 10
a.m. to 5 p.m. daily (noon to 5 p.m. Sunday); closed Good Friday
and Christmas. Free admission.
● **Royal Botanic Gardens**—The second botanic gardens in the
Southern Hemisphere are a pleasant place for a stroll or a picnic.
Open 8 a.m. to sunset daily. Free guided walks are conducted at
9:30 a.m. Wednesday and 10 a.m. Friday from the visitor centre.
●● **The Australian Museum**—Corner William and College
Streets (opposite Hyde Park). This museum is of special interest
for superb exhibits of Aboriginal and Papua New Guinean
lifestyles. It also has good displays of Australian geological and
natural history. In 1988, a Pacific art gallery and other new
exhibits were opened. Open 10 a.m. to 5 p.m. daily (noon to 5
p.m. Monday); closed Good Friday and Christmas. Free
admission.
●● **Powerhouse Museum**—Harris and Mary Ann Streets,
Ultimo. A highly acclaimed new science and technology museum
opened for the Bicentennial in 1988, this features everything from
steam engines to the space race to the history of the brewing
industry in New South Wales. Many displays are hands-on. Open
10 a.m. to 5 p.m. daily.
●● **Darling Harbour**—This urban reclamation project on the
west end of central Sydney is 'the place to go'. In addition to a
hotel/casino and convention centre, it includes eight waterfront
restaurants and cafes, 100 retail shops, night clubs, a maritime
museum and aquarium, a Chinese garden and a waterfront
promenade. A monorail connects Darling Harbour to the city
centre.
● **Elizabeth Bay House**—Onslow Avenue, Elizabeth Bay. Close
to Kings Cross but on the Sydney Explorer bus route, this
elegant 1835 colonial mansion has been fully restored to period
decor. Open 10 a.m. to 4:30 p.m. Tuesday to Sunday. Adult
admission $2.50 (£1.20); Sydney Explorer patrons $2 (95p).
●●● **The Rocks**—Sydney's most historic district is located just
northwest of Circular Quay. The oldest building still standing,
Cadmans Cottage, was built in 1816, but most structures date
from the 1840s to 1880s, during which time this was Sydney's
main commercial and maritime quarter.
    To see the area properly, you should guide yourself on a walk-
ing tour beginning from The Rocks Visitor Centre, 104 George
Street—open Monday to Friday 8:30 a.m. to 4:30 p.m., weekends

and holidays 10 a.m. to 5 p.m. You can pick up a map describing various sites, but the best way to explore is simply to amble and browse, ducking into the various small shops, art galleries, museums and pubs. Several pubs, including The Old Push, Phillips Foote and the venerable Hero of Waterloo, feature live 'trad jazz' performances during after-work 'happy hour' and on weekends.

The highlight of The Rocks is the **Argyle Centre,** a four-storey complex of various artisans' galleries, antique shops and cafes. Housed in a group of 1828 sandstone bond stores and warehouses, it authentically preserves the atmosphere of the period—and nowhere better than the **Argyle Tavern,** a great spot for an Australian night out. As you fill up on Sydney rock oysters, grilled barramundi or steak-and-kidney pie, the Jolly Swagman Show will introduce you to a variety of Aussie bush ballads and folk songs, the Aboriginal didgeridoo (a primitive droning instrument) and the fine art of shearing a sheep...right on stage. Showtime is 8 to 9:30 nightly; come by 7:30 to place your order and beat the rush. A warning: shoe-string travellers may want to think twice before purging their wallets of A$42.50 (£20) (per person) for the dinner and show.

TOUR 3

MORE OF SYDNEY

I'd spend today touring the Eastern Suburbs, but there are many
other options—take the ferry to Manly and the zoo, for instance,
or travel to the Blue Mountains or the Hunter Valley.

Suggested schedule

9:00 a.m.	Take the subway (Blue Line) to Bondi Junction, then catch Bus No. 380 or 389 to Bondi Beach. You'll arrive by 9:30 a.m., giving you two hours to soak in rays and surf culture before lunch.
11:30 a.m.	Catch a city bus north up the coast to Watson's Bay for a seafood lunch at Doyle's.
1:30 p.m.	Bus No. 325 heads back toward the city. Stop off at Vaucluse House, an 1830s mansion.
2:30 p.m.	Disembark in Double Bay for a look at Sydney's fashionable area.
3:30 p.m.	Have a taxi drop you in Paddington at the New Edition Bookshop, 328 Oxford St, where you can obtain free 'The Paddington Book' with a map and suggested walking tour.
5:30 p.m.	Continue to the Cross by foot, bus or taxi. It's your night to paint the town red.

Sightseeing highlights

● ● **Bondi** (pronounced Bond-eye)—It is the most famous of all
Sydney's beaches. It's not the most attractive, unless perhaps
you're talking about the topless south end of the beach; but there
seems to be more tradition and a livelier crowd here than at other
Eastern Suburbs beaches, especially during summer when surf
lifesaving contests are held throughout Australia.
● **Vaucluse House**—Olala Avenue, Vaucluse, was built in 1803
and became the home of William Charles Wentworth. A
beachfront manor which sits in 27 acres of park and garden, it
has been lavishly refurbished in the style of Wentworth's time.
Open 10 a.m. to 4:30 p.m. Tuesday to Sunday. Adult admission
is $2.50 (£1.20).
● **Double Bay**—May be Australia's most fashionable few streets.
Knox Street, Cross Street and New South Head Road are lined

with designer boutiques, exclusive jewellers and antique shops.
You'll see Sydney's beautiful people sizing each other up at
pavement cafes and delis.

●● **Paddington**—May be downmarket from Double Bay, but it's
upmarket from most of the rest of Sydney. Known locally as
'Paddo' this hilly neighbourhood might strike Londoners as being
a little like Clapham. Here, the young, upwardly mobile
population has put its restoration energies into Victorian terrace
houses rather than brownstone manors. Many artists, musicians
and educators live among the trendy arts and crafts galleries and
numerous fine restaurants and pubs.

Special attractions in Paddington include an open-air market
called the **Village Bazaar**, held from 9 a.m. to 4 p.m. every
Saturday at the corner of Newcombe and Oxford Streets, and the
Victoria Barracks, a superb example of British colonial military
architecture on Oxford Street opposite Hopewell Street. If you're
here on Tuesday, see the impressive changing of the guard at 11
a.m.

● **Manley**—Is a good destination for those who prefer to spend
time on the water instead of in trains and buses. Spread across a
narrow neck of land separating the Harbour from the Tasman
Sea, it has a quaint pedestrian precinct connecting the famed surfing beach with a still-water swimming area. Manly's attractions
include a Marineland (open 10 a.m. to 5 p.m. daily), an
amusement pier, a series of waterslides, and an art
gallery/museum. Manly is easily reached from Circular Quay by
ferry (A$1.30 (60p) each way) or hydrofoil (A$2.40 (£1.15) each
way).

● **Taronga Park Zoo**—Bradleys Head Road, Mosman, is an
excellent place to get an introduction to Australia's unique
wildlife. Its exhibits include a treetop koala exhibit, a platypus
house, a rainforest aviary and a special nocturnal house. You can
travel there either by ferry from Circular Quay (A$1 (45p) each
way) or by Bus No. 237 or 238 across the Sydney Harbour
Bridge. Open daily year-round, 9 a.m. to 5 p.m. Admission is $5
(£2.40).

Birkenhead Point—A shopping centre off Victoria Road in the
harbourside suburb of Drummoyne, a few miles west of the city
centre, might be considered a rainy-day option. There are some
130 shops and restaurants, plus the **Lego Centre**, one of only
two permanent exhibitions in the world of models built from
these children's building blocks. Open daily 9:15 a.m. to 5:15
p.m., Thursdays until 9 p.m.

The **Sydney Maritime Museum**, with a fleet of historic
ships, is also located here. It's open Monday 1:30 to 5 p.m.,
Tuesday to Friday 10 a.m. to 5 p.m., Saturday and Sunday 11:30

a.m. to 4:30 p.m. Birkenhead Point is reached by bus No. 500 or 502 from Circular Quay to the Iron Cove Bridge.

Day trips from Sydney

If you're inclined to hire your car a day early, here are some worthwhile day trip options.

● **The Blue Mountains**—Once a foreboding natural barrier to early settlers, they are now a favourite weekend getaway for Sydneysiders. Their undeclared capital is Katoomba, a small town 106 km (66 miles) west of Sydney, though they spread from Penrith to Lithgow. The mountains' most famous attraction is **The Three Sisters,** an unusual rock formation associated with Aboriginal legend. A cablecar and scenic railway at the site make it a honeymooners' delight. There are also spectacular caves and waterfalls, art galleries and historic museums.

● **Pittwater and Broken Bay**—At the mouth of the Hawkesbury River marking the northern boundary of the Sydney metropolis, these are places of great natural beauty. They're best seen from the deck of a private yacht, but they can also be thoroughly appreciated from the land. Drive north up Sydney's east coast through Mona Vale to **Palm Beach**, or better yet, spend an afternoon bushwalking in **Ku-ring-gai Chase National Park.**

● **Old Sydney Town**—Near Gosford about 70 km (43 miles) north of central Sydney, this recreates the Sydney Cove settlement as it is thought to have been in the early 19th century. Only authentic materials and methods were used in building the 50-acre theme park. Soldiers, convicts and free settlers, all in period costume, continually act out scenes from the colony's history. Open 10 a.m. to 5 p.m. Wednesday to Sunday; daily during school holidays. Admission is $8.50 (£4). A rail tour, leaving Sydney's Central Station at 9:15 a.m. and returning shortly after 6:30 p.m., costs $20 (£9.50) for adults and includes admission.

● **The Hunter Valley**—Near Cessnock some 180 km (110 miles) north of Sydney, this is Australia's oldest wine-producing district and its second most important (after the Barossa Valley near Adelaide). The 34 wineries here are best known for their soft reds. Most are open for tasting daily from 9 or 10 a.m. to about 5 p.m. Hungerford Hill, Rothbury Estate, Tyrrells and Wyndham Estate are among the most highly regarded.

Night life

Anything and everything goes in **Kings Cross**, several meandering blocks of burlesque shows, theatre restaurants, discotheques, tattoo parlours and streetwalkers where Darlinghurst

Road, Victoria Street, Bayswater Road and William Street come together a mile east of the city centre. Some call the Cross 'bohemian', others 'sleazy'; the truth may lie somewhere between. People-watching is the best form of entertainment here; grab a window table and a cup of capuccino at an open-air cafe. You might also get a kick out of the automated Ray Charles double playing piano and singing at **Jo Jo Ivory's** in the Potts Point Sheraton, 40 Macleay Street.

To find out what's happening on any given day in the greater Sydney area, get hold of *The Sydney Morning Herald's* Friday 'Metro' section, with listings of the entertainment week ahead. Musical offerings are broken down into classical, jazz, country, folk, acoustic and rock, with the latter category as large as the other five combined. Paddington (try the **Grand National Hotel** or the **Windsor Castle Hotel**) and Bondi (the **Royal Hotel** is best) have especially large concentrations of music pubs, but you'll find them everywhere.

The best modern jazz in Sydney is consistently found at **The Basement**, 29 Reiby Place near Circular Quay.

If you're strictly into meeting people without having to shout over the din of music, check out some of the city's wine bars— like **French's** on Oxford Street in Darlinghurst, **Soren's** in Woolloomooloo or **The Stoned Crow** in Crow's Nest, across the Harbour Bridge. In North Sydney you'll also find **Sheila's**, a singles bar with provocative coasters that read: 'If you're looking for a friend, leave this side up'.

Live theatre is extremely popular in Sydney. Aside from the Opera House, you can watch fine productions at **The Theatre Royal** on King Street, **The Wharf Theatre** on Pier 4 (near The Rocks), the **Nimrod Theatre** in Chippendale and others.

Lower George Street has the greatest concentration of cinema houses for moviegoers. All major-studio foreign films are shown here, but don't miss an opportunity to see some of the outstanding films made in Australia today.

An Australian phenomenon is the Leagues Club, of which rugby league clubs and returned servicemen's league clubs are most prevalent. Depending upon their size, they usually include a small gambling casino (with slot machines), a restaurant and bar, and an entertainment lounge, often with live music on weekends. This is where the working man typically takes his wife or girlfriend for a night out. While they are membership clubs, overseas visitors are normally welcome. Two of the biggest are the **South Sydney Junior Rugby League Club**, 556 Anzac Parade, Kingsford, and the **St George Leagues Club**, 124 Princes Highway, Kogarah.

TOUR 4

SYDNEY TO CANBERRA

Leave Australia's queen city and drive south to Canberra, the
national capital, pausing en route at historic Gledswood
Homestead and Berrima. In Canberra, take time for an overview
of the foundation and continuing evolution of this attractive,
specially created city.

Suggested schedule

8:00 a.m.	Pick up your reserved hire car and head out of Sydney via the Hume Highway.
9:30 a.m.	Arrive at Gledswood Homestead and wander through the working colonial farm.
10:45 a.m.	Leave for Berrima.
11:30 a.m.	Explore Berrima, a sandstone-and-brick village appearing very much today as it did in 1831. Lunch at the Surveyor General Inn, the oldest continuously licensed pub in Australia.
1:30 p.m.	Leave for Canberra.
3:30 p.m.	On arrival, drive straight to the Regatta Point Planning Exhibition on Lake Burley Griffin. Study the models and see the video to understand the grand plan for this 20th century capital.
4:30 p.m.	Capture the view from the top of Mount Ainslie.
5:00 p.m.	Move into your accommodation. Plan on a quiet evening; most of them are just that in Canberra.

Leaving Sydney

When you obtain your hire car, double-check to be certain your
agent has provided you with a Gregory's or UBD street guide to
Sydney. That's your passport out of the metropolis in case you
get lost.

Most visitors get their car at an agency on William Street,
between Kings Cross and the centre. Proceed west through Hyde
Park, turn left on Pitt Street and follow the signs to Liverpool.
The Hume Highway, Route 31, branches south (to the left) off
the Great Western Highway near Summer Hill, 8 km from
William Street.

The Hume Highway

Soon after leaving Liverpool, about 30 km from the Hume
Highway junction, the highway becomes a four-lane motorway. It
stays that way (with only a couple of slowdowns) all the way to
Canberra—in fact, to Melbourne—enabling you to drive the 294
km (183 miles) from Sydney to the capital in 3½ hours, if you so
chose.

Our tour route, however, involves a few diversions. At the
point where the motorway begins, turn right on Route 89,
Camden Valley Way (the old Hume Highway), to the community
of Catherine Field. It's about 10 km further to the historic
Gledswood Homestead, built in 1810 by convict labour and
now classified by the Australian National Trust and the Heritage
Commission. Guided tours of the homestead, winery (in a former
coach house) and working farm are offered daily from 9 a.m. to 5
p.m. Sheep shearing, boomerang throwing and other
demonstrations are often presented.

●● **Berrima** has recently been bypassed by the new motorway,
making its colonial isolation all the more appealing. Situated
128 km (80 miles) from Sydney and 166 km (103 miles) from
Canberra, this village (founded in 1831) is a historical gem. Pick
up a walking tour map at the Georgian-style **courthouse**, where
the first jury trial in the New South Wales colony was held in
1843. (It's open 10 a.m. to 4 p.m. daily; admission is 60 cents
(28p).) The **gaol**, built in 1839, closed in 1902 but reopened in
1949 after extensive reconstruction (and still in use), was one of
the most feared in Australia in the mid-19th century.

About two dozen government buildings, early churches and
private manors have survived the passage of time. Many of them
may contain galleries, antique and crafts shops, restaurants and
cafés serving Devonshire teas. At the **Surveyor General Inn**,
which celebrated its 155th anniversary in business in 1989, you
can cook your own steak lunch, pile it high with a salad bar and
potatoes, and wash it down with a beer for under A$10 (£4.75).

A further diversion off the Hume Highway from Berrima would
lead you through the charming village of **Bundanoon** at the edge
of lush Morton National Park. Time's a-wastin', however. Return
to the motorway, drive right on through the big farming centre of
Goulburn (pop. 25,000), waving at the ridiculous 'world's largest
Merino sheep' sculpture as you pass. Twelve km further on, bear
left onto the Federal Highway and slide by the rim of large (but
usually dry) Lake George into the Australian Capital Territory.

Canberra orientation

Visitors often find Canberra like a tree without roots, a building
without a foundation. Indeed, the city is too young to have

developed much heritage of its own. Like Washington, DC, Canberra, ACT, is strictly a government town—but its 250,000 people haven't had a long enough history to develop a feeling of heritage. It wasn't until 1901 that Melbourne and Sydney, throwing up their political arms in frustration over persistent squabbling for the right to be the national capital, finally compromised and agreed to construct a new city between the two metropolises.

In 1912, an American architect named Walter Burley Griffin won an international contest to design the capital. Following his plans, 2,366 square km (913 square miles) of sheep-grazing land was transformed into the Australian Capital Territory, and within that plot, the new city of Canberra was built. (The name 'Canberra' was derived from an Aboriginal term meaning 'meeting place'.) In 1927, all government functions were moved here from Melbourne.

Burley Griffin's grandiose plan has taken far longer to complete than anyone imagined. Between two world wars, a Great Depression and much political in-fighting, construction funds have been hard to come by. At the time of writing, in fact, Canberra is still not completed to the architect's specifications! After 60 years of legislative debates in a provisional parliament house, a magnificent new Parliament House was finished just in time for the Australian Bicentennial in 1988.

Canberra's design carefully balances natural features—low, bush-cloaked mountains and lovely, meandering Lake Burley Griffin—with geometrical patterns, mainly a series of concentric circles interconnected by strong lines. Capital Hill, site of the new Parliament, and City Hill, around which most commercial functions revolve, are 3 km apart, linked across the deep blue lake by Commonwealth Avenue. Each 'hill' is the hub of a series of streets which spread from the centre like the spokes of a wheel.

Northbourne Avenue, on which you'll arrive from the north, runs straight as an arrow for over 4 km directly to City Hill. Soon after you circumnavigate the hill, but before crossing the lake, look for directional signs to the **Canberra Planning Exhibition** on Regatta Point, operated by the National Capital Development Commission. Put preconceived notions aside; if you have any interest in the creative process, it isn't boring. In effect it's a historical museum, describing with text, photographs and audiovisual presentation the creation of Canberra from virtually uninhabited bush. A huge three-dimensional model of the city helps you locate points of interest. Open 9 a.m. to 5 p.m. daily (except Christmas); admission is free. A snack bar and souvenir shop are on a terrace overlooking the lake.

Of several hills with lookouts over the city, the best—from the standpoint of understanding Canberra's layout—is **Mount Ainslie** in the northeast quadrant. Not only is it the highest at 842 metres (2,772 feet); from the top, you can look straight down across the stalwart Australian War Memorial to Anzac Parade, which neatly bisects the Federal Triangle and affords a direct view of the provisional and new Parliament Houses.

The highest viewpoint in Canberra is actually atop the striking 195-metre (640-foot) Telecom Tower on **Black Mountain** west of City Hill. But unless you dine in the revolving restaurant, you'll have to pay to gain access to the three public viewing galleries. Another lookout is on **Red Hill**, south of Capital Hill, with a restaurant offering panoramic views of the southern suburbs.

Canberra's climate, quite logically, is unlike that of any of the seaside state capitals. Located about 120 km (75 miles) inland and at 580 metres (1,900 feet) elevation in a spur of the Great Dividing Range, its summers are hotter and drier than other major cities and its winters colder, with occasional (if rare) snow flurries.

City transport

If you arrive in Canberra without a car at the airport, railway depot or bus station, you're not stranded. The ACTION public bus network runs through the city and its suburbs from 6 a.m. to 11:30 p.m. daily (8:30 a.m. to 6:30 p.m. Sunday), with fares of 60 cents (28p) to most destinations. No. 230 operates to Regatta Point and along the north shore of Lake Burley Griffin; No. 302 runs from the city to the Australian War Memorial; No. 357 connects City Hill with the rail station via the National Library and provisional Parliament House; No. 380 plies the 8 km (five miles) between the youth hostel and the centre.

Better designed for the tourist is the **Canberra Explorer.** This unmistakable bright red bus runs its narrated 25-km (15½-mile) circuit seven times every day from 9:40 a.m. to 4:35 p.m., making scheduled stops at major attractions and hotels. You can buy a day ticket for $7 (£3.35), allowing you to disembark anywhere and reboard an hour or two later, or pay $2.50 (£1.20) for a one-hour tour.

Where to stay

The greatest concentration of accommodation in all price categories is along Northbourne Avenue, the main thoroughfare entering Canberra from the north. Regarded by some as the best is the **Canberra International**, 242 Northbourne Avenue, Dickson, ACT 2602 (tel. 47-6966), with luxury rooms and a garden atmosphere. I'm happy in the moderate price range at **Down Town Spero's Motel**, 82 Northbourne Avenue,

Canberra, ACT 2601 (tel. 49-1388), an easy three-street stroll
from the commercial centre around City Hill.

You'll find adequate economy-class lodging at **Tall Trees
Lodge**, Stephen and Sherbrooke Streets, Ainslie, ACT 2602 (tel.
47-9200). The **Gowrie Private Hotel**, 210 Northbourne Avenue,
Braddon, ACT 2602 (tel. 49-6033), has twin 10-storey towers
containing 569 simple rooms and a big ground floor cafeteria.

True budget accommodation is hard to come by in Canberra,
but the **National Memorial Youth Hostel** is on Dryandra
Street in O'Connor, ACT 2601 (tel. 48-9759).

Where to eat

The most central area for dining is Garema Place, a spacious
pedestrian precinct east of Northbourne Avenue and north of
London Circuit, just above City Hill. There's a wide range of
choices here, from candlelit meals to fast-food takeaway.
Dorette's Bistro, upstairs at 17 Garema Place (near Bunda
Street), is one of my favourites; it's a self-styled Bohemian cafe
with live classical and jazz music on alternate nights. **Mama's
Trattoria**, 7 Garema Place, offers big pasta meals for no more
than A$7 (£3.35). A couple of streets away is the 24-hour **Lovely
Lady Pancake Parlour**, East Row and Alinga Street, with full
meals A$5 – $7 (£2.35 – £3.35) and a bottomless coffee cup. Not
far away, near City Hill on Northbourne Avenue, **Boyd's Cafe**
at No. 47 and the **Private Bin** at No. 50 offer bistro menus and
entertainment. Vegetarians congregate at the **Honeydew
Wholemeal**, 55 Northbourne Avenue.

In the centre, upmarket favourites among politicians and local
businessmen are the **Fringe Benefits** brasserie, 54 Marcus
Clarke Street, and **Seasons**, in the Canberra Theatre Centre,
both serving continental cuisine.

Not far from Garema Place, on Lonsdale Street, **The Eureka
Stockade** at No. 17 is a local favourite for steaks and beer.
Opposite at No. 14 – 16 are the **Siamese Kitchen**, with spicy
Southeast Asian cuisine for $8 to $10 (£3.80 – £4.75), and the
Tipsy Gypsy, a Hungarian restaurant. Other ethnic restaurants
in the Civic Centre area include Chinese, Indian, Vietnamese and
Lebanese.

Worthy of special note are **Tilley Devine's Cafe Gallery**, 96
Wattle Street, Lynehan, a feminist-operated establishment which
doesn't admit men unless accompanied by women; the **Tau**, on
Mort Street directly behind Spero's, a vegetarian and Middle
Eastern restaurant operated by a community theatre group; the
Canberra Tradesmen's Union Club, Badham Street, Dickson,
with reasonably priced bistro meals served in restored trams; and
a pair of cafeterias in Australian National University's student

centre, the **ANU Refectory** and the **Asian Bistro**.

Helpful hints

The **Canberra Tourist Bureau** (tel. 45-6405 or 45-6464) has its
main offices in the Jolimont Centre on Northbourne Avenue near
London Circuit. It's open weekdays 8:30 a.m. to 5:15 p.m. and
Saturdays 9 to 11:30 a.m. More convenient for those driving into
town from the north is the **Visitor Information Centre**, on
Northbourne Avenue just south of the junctions of the Federal
and Barton highways, open daily (except Christmas) from 9 a.m.
to 5 p.m.

The **General Post Office** adjoins the Jolimont Centre at
Alinga and Moore streets. Banks open from 9:30 a.m. to 4 p.m.
Monday to Thursday, an hour later on Friday. Shops are
generally open 9 a.m. to 5:30 p.m. Monday to Friday, 9 a.m. to
4 p.m. Saturday. (Some stay open later Friday nights but close by
noon Saturday.)

The **British High Commission** is situated on Commonwealth
Avenue, Canberra ACT 2601.

In case of emergencies, dial 000.

TOUR 5

CANBERRA

Explore the national capital. Start at the new Parliament House; if the Senate and House of Representatives are in session, you can view the proceedings from a public gallery. Take a drive through the Yarralumla area to see the impressive row of national embassies, then lunch at the High Court, inspect the National Gallery and visit the Australian War Memorial museum.

Suggested schedule

9:00 a.m.	View Australia's new Parliament House.
9:30 a.m.	Queue up for a 10:00 a.m. session of the Senate or House of Representatives at the new Parliament House.
11:00 a.m.	Drive through Canberra's 'Embassy Row'.
12:00 noon	Visit the High Court and have lunch in its café.
1:30 p.m.	Peruse the Australian National Gallery.
3:00 p.m.	Spend a couple of hours at the Australian War Memorial Museum.
5:00 p.m.	Hire a canoe for a trip on Lake Burley Griffin or return to your hotel and relax.
7:00 p.m.	Dine in Garema Place.

Sightseeing highlights

● ● ● **The New Parliament House**—With its unmistakable A$4 million (£1.9 million) flagpole, officially opened on 9 May 1988. The designers — the American firm of Mitchell/Giurgola and Australian architect Richard Thorp—kept intact Walter Burley Griffin's original plan for Canberra with gently curving walls and careful landscaping picking up the axis pattern of earlier roads and buildings. The 266-foot, four-legged flagpole is now the emblem of Australian government. Excavation of the site began in 1981; the final cost is estimated at over A$1 billion (£475 million).

● ● ● **The Provisional Parliament House**—The seat of Australia's federal government since 1927. A graceful white building in a park-like setting on King George Terrace, it hosted the Senate and House of Representatives for the final time in early 1988.

At the time of writing the Provisional House was still partially in use, though once all proceedings have been transferred to the

New Parliament House it is likely to close for renovation. Its
future use still seems uncertain though it may continue as an art
gallery. Check with the Canberra Tourist Bureau (tel. 45-6405 or
45-6464) in advance.

●● **The High Court of Australia**—In an impressive concrete-
and-glass structure on the shore of Lake Burley Griffin, is the
nation's ultimate court of appeal. The Great Hall—the main
public area—has two huge murals depicting the justice system and
the states. Ramps connect it with courtrooms on three succeeding
floors, decorated with indigenous woodwork, woven tapestries,
sculptures and other native artworks. When in session, the court
sits from 10:15 a.m. to 12:45 p.m. and 2:15 to 4:15 p.m.
weekdays. The building is open to visitors 9:45 a.m. to 4:30 p.m.
most days. A licensed café, overlooking Lake Burley Griffin,
serves excellent light meals for A$5 or less (£2.35).

●● **The Australian National Gallery**—Connected by a first-
floor walkway to the High Court building, has a fine if limited
collection of Australian and foreign paintings, sculpture and
decorative arts. Free guided tours of the Australian art section are
offered daily at 11:15 a.m. and 2:15 p.m. The gallery is open 10
a.m. to 5 p.m. daily except Good Friday and Christmas;
admission is $2 (95p).

●● **The National Library of Australia**—West of the High
Court on the lakefront, has an Australian art collection of its own,
displayed daily from 9 a.m. to 4:45 p.m. in the Rex Nan Kivell
Room. Some 3.6 million volumes of books are stored in 10 acres
of space and on 47 miles of shelves. The main reading room is
open to the public 9:30 a.m. to 10 p.m. Monday to Thursday,
9:30 a.m. to 4:45 p.m. Friday and Saturday, and 1:30 to 4:45
p.m. Sunday.

●●● **The Australian War Memorial**—Is the country's best
museum of any kind. Whether you view war as glorious, horrible
or a bit of both, this sombre memorial will make a definite
impression. Inscribed with the names of more than 102,000
Australians who died in service to their country, it stares straight
down tree-lined Anzac Parade and across Lake Burley Griffin at
Parliament House, 4 km (2½ miles) distant. Built in the 1930s
and expanded often since, the museum/art gallery traces Aussie
military history from British colonial times through the First
World War tragedy of Gallipoli and the Second World War
attacks on Darwin to Australia's more modern involvement in the
Vietnam conflict. Free guided tours are available weekdays at
10:30 a.m. and 1:30 p.m. Open daily 9 a.m. to 4:45 p.m. Free
admission.

● **Lake Burley Griffin**—The vivid blue centrepiece of Canberra,
is highlighted by the Captain Cook Memorial Water Jet (sending

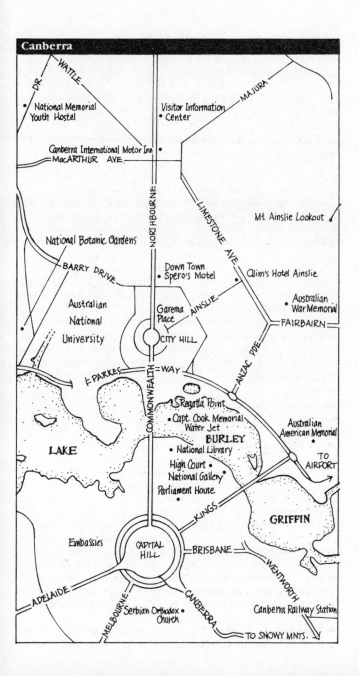

Canberra

National Memorial Youth Hostel

Visitor Information Center

Canberra International Motor Inn
MacARTHUR AVE.

Mt. Ainslie Lookout

National Botanic Gardens

BARRY DRIVE

Down Town
Spero's Motel

Qlim's Hotel Ainslie

Australian War Memorial

FAIRBAIRN

Australian National University

Garema Place

AINSLIE

CITY HILL

E PARKES WAY

COMMONWEALTH

NORTHBOURNE

LIMESTONE AVE.

MAJURA

WATTLE
DR.

ANZAC PDE.

Regatta Point

Capt. Cook Memorial Water Jet

BURLEY

National Library

High Court
National Gallery
Parliament House

Australian American Memorial

TO AIRPORT

LAKE

KINGS

GRIFFIN

Embassies

CAPITAL HILL

BRISBANE

WENTWORTH

ADELAIDE

MELBOURNE

Serbian Orthodox Church

CANBERRA

Canberra Railway Station

TO SNOWY MNTS.

a column of water 430 feet above the lake from 10 a.m. to noon
and again 2 to 4 p.m. daily) and the Carillon (a 53-bell tower
with free recitals on Wednesdays, Sundays and holidays). You can
cruise the lake for an hour or two aboard the 'City of Canberra'
or 'Lady Claire' (leaving at noon and 1 p.m. daily, cost A$6 to $9
(£2.85 to £4.25)), or hire a rowing boat, canoe, paddleboat or
windsurfer (A$7 to $10 an hour (£3.35 to £4.75)). All water
activities are centred on West Basin in Acton Park.

Nightlife

Canberra's evening activity is pretty tame. **Juliana's**, in Noah's
Lakeside International Hotel on London Circuit, is the top
discotheque; **Dorette's Bistro** is good for light classical and jazz.
Things liven up a bit on Friday and Saturday night, when several
small bars and taverns feature live entertainment for dancing.
Most residents find their diversions at RSL, leagues or other
clubs in Canberra or neighbouring Queanbeyan, NSW. Visitors
are welcome; check out the **Canberra Labour Club**, Chandler
Street in Belconnen; the **Canberra Workers Club**, University
Avenue and Children's Street, City; or the **Royals Rugby Union
Football Club**, Weston Creek.

The modern **Canberra Theatre Centre** in Civic Square, off
London Circuit, contains a theatre, playhouse, gallery, restaurant
and rehearsal room. Everything from serious drama to world-class
ballet to Gilbert and Sullivan to rock concerts is presented here.
Call the box office (tel. 57-1077) for current offerings and prices.

TOUR 6

CANBERRA TO BEECHWORTH

Today's route leads past the alpine resort of Thredbo in the Snowy Mountains; via Corryong, reputed home of poet Banjo Paterson's 'Man from Snowy River'; to Beechworth, a town straight out of the 19th century gold-rush era.

Suggested schedule

8:30 a.m.	Leave Canberra, driving via Cooma to Thredbo.
11:30 a.m.	Arrive at Thredbo. Take an hour for lunch and a look around, or buy some food for sandwiches and stop for a picnic further down the road.
2:30 p.m.	After a drive down the Alpine Way through the Snowy Mountains, visit tiny Corryong to see the Man from Snowy River Folk Museum.
4:30 p.m.	Arrive in Yackandandah, for a short tour of this village classified by the National Trust.
5:30 p.m.	Reach the fascinating town of Beechworth, whose main street has changed little in 100 years.

Today's drive

Follow the signs off Canberra Avenue, southeast of Capital Hill, to reach the Monaro Highway. **Cooma**, 117 km (73 miles) south of Canberra, is about a 1½ hour drive. Often considered the 'gateway' to the Snowy Mountains because most skiers pass through it en route to the various resorts, this town of 8,000 also is headquarters of the Snowy Mountains Hydro-Electric Scheme, a massive project which created dams, power stations and high-altitude lakes throughout the range west of here.

Thredbo, another 96 km (53 miles) of winding road west across the Snowy River, is built like a Tyrolean village with chalets dotting its alpine slopes. Regarded as Australia's No. 1 ski resort, it is also a popular summer escape with the country's highest golf course (1,370m or 4,495 feet), tennis courts and horse riding trails. Looming above the snowfields at the top of its Crackenback chairlift is Australia's highest peak, Mount Kosciusko, 2,229m (7,313) feet in elevation. It's an easy walk for summer day-hikers and winter 'langlaufers', cross-country skiers. Non-skiers find spring the best time to visit, when the slopes are

covered with wildflowers. Twenty separate lodges and a youth
hostel provide beds and/or meals for skiers and other holiday-
makers. The Thredbo Alpine Hotel, at the foot of the mountain,
is a good choice for lunch with a view.

Alpine Way runs for 74 km (46 miles) through Kosciusko
National Park from Thredbo to Khancoban. More than half of
the route is gravel, but it's well-graded and is not normally (snow
or heavy rain excepted) a difficult or dangerous drive. On the
other hand, it's tremendously scenic, offering numerous vistas of
the dense bush surrounding the headwaters of the Murray River,
Australia's longest. On the off-chance you've thrown a fishing
pole in with your gear, the streams and lakes along this road are a
good place to cast a line. Buy a licence as you pass through
Cooma (A$5 (£2.35) for 30 days).

Upon reaching **Khancoban**, a tiny township established for
hydro-electric workers, you will have dropped nearly 3,500 feet
from Thredbo. Follow the signs across the Murray River into the
state of Victoria. It's 21 km (13 miles) to **Corryong**.

A broad main street establishes the character of this country
centre. If you didn't see the film starring Kirk Douglas and
several Australian actors, be sure to read Banjo Paterson's short
but stirring ballad, 'The Man from Snowy River', before you
arrive. Jack Riley, generally regarded as the model for the poem,
made his home in Corryong and is buried in the town cemetery.
He and his legend are remembered at the **Man from Snowy
River Folk Museum** with an eclectic but charming variety of
exhibits including skis used by 19th century gold miners. Located
at the west end of town, it's open only from 2 to 3 p.m. Monday
to Saturday. Admission is $2 (95p).

Rather than backtracking on the Murray Valley Highway,
proceed directly west about 120 km (75 miles) via Tallangatta to
Yackandandah. (You can avoid the bottleneck of the Albury-
Wodonga area by cutting over to the Kiewa Valley Highway near
Tangambalanga.) So important is Yackandandah, historically and
architecturally, that the entire township and surrounding hills are
classified by the National Trust. Why the hills? Because the
creeks and 19th century gold diggings still yield alluvial gold to
amateur prospectors.

Beechworth

The most historically interesting town in northeast Victoria is
Beechworth, 24 km (15 miles) southwest of Yackandandah.
Established in 1839, it soon became one of Australia's richest
goldfields, yielding 4.1 million ounces between 1852 and 1862.
Commercial mining continued until 1920, and weekend panners
still find gold in the creeks today.

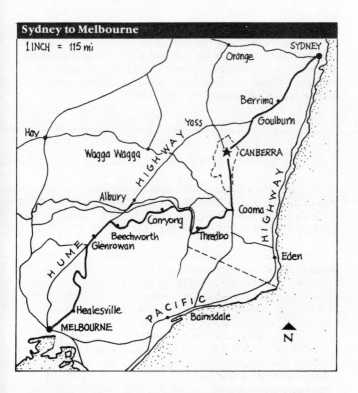

Sydney to Melbourne

1 INCH = 115 mi

By the time you arrive, the visitor information centre in The Rock Cavern, at Ford and Camp Streets, will probably be closed. You can take a 'formal' self-guided tour tomorrow morning. For now, check into accommodation with appropriate 19th century atmosphere, dine and get some sleep.

Rose Cottage Bed and Breakfast, 42 Camp Street (tel. 057/28-1069), is a quaint four-bedroom home fully furnished with Victorian antiques. The price of A$36 (£17) single, A$49 (£23) double includes a full breakfast. Next door, the more common-place but comfortable **Carriage Motor Inn**, 44 Camp Street (tel. 28-1830), charges A$34 (£16) single, A$40 (£19) double.

Transwell's Commercial Hotel, 30 Ford Street (tel. 28-1480), 118 years old, has 'toilets-down-the-hall' rooms for A$25 (£12) single, A$35 (£16.50) double, including breakfast. (Superb dinners are priced from A$9.50 (£4.50) in the restaurant, and the pub serves A$6 (£2.85) counter meals.) The **Empire Hotel**, Camp and High Streets (tel. 28-1030), has a similar set-up with adequate rooms for A$15 (£7.15) single, A$25 (£12) double.

Across the street from Transwell's, the **Youth Hostel** (tel. 28-1425) is housed in the old Star Hotel.

Aside from Transwell's you can dine well over the counter at any of the town's four pubs. There's a Chinese restaurant, the **Chinese Village**, on Camp Street, and many travellers enjoy **Rosemary's Coffee Shop** on Ford Street.

TOUR 7

BEECHWORTH TO MELBOURNE

After a morning tour of Beechworth, we'll visit the Brown Brothers Winery at Milawa and stop in at Glenrowan, where Ned Kelly, Australia's most notorious 19th century bushranger, made his 'last stand'. The afternoon's highlight is the Sir Colin McKenzie Wildlife Sanctuary, an open-air reserve at Healesville that is the best of its kind in the world. Arrive in Melbourne in time for dinner.

Suggested schedule

8:00 a.m.	Breakfast in Beechworth, then explore the town and museum until about 10:30.
11:00 a.m.	Tour Brown Brothers Winery and sample the product.
11:45 a.m.	Dive into 'Kelly Country' at the museums and roadside display in Glenrowan.
12:30 p.m.	Grab picnic goodies in Benalla and enjoy them on the banks of Lake Nillahcootie.
3:00 p.m.	Stroll for two hours among native Australian wildlife at the Sir Colin McKenzie Wildlife Sanctuary at Healesville.
6:30 p.m.	Arrive in Melbourne. Check into your hotel and head for a well-earned dinner on Lygon Street.

Beechworth sightseeing highlights

No fewer than 32 of Beechworth's buildings have been classified or recorded by the Australian National Trust. The best place to start your exploration is the **Burke Memorial Museum**, on Loch Street just north of Camp Street. Established at this site in 1863, it is one of Australia's finest small-town museums. The collection is especially strong in pioneer history, the goldrush era, and memorabilia of the local Chinese community and the Kelly Gang. A new gallery reproduces a 16-shop main street of the mid-19th century with retail shops, a doctor's office, an assay office, a dance hall and other establishments. Open 2 to 4:30 p.m. Monday, 11 a.m. to 4:30 p.m. Friday, 9 a.m. to 4:30 p.m. all other days. Admission is A$2 (95p).

On leaving the Burke Museum, pick up a copy of the

lithographed brochure, 'Beechworth Living History'. Its map will
direct you to 34 points of interest in the Beechworth area, most
of them within easy walking distance. Among the properties
administered by the National Trust are the **Carriage Museum**,
behind Transwell's Hotel, with an extensive collection of carriages
and other turn-of-the-century vehicles, and the **Powder
Magazine**, on Gorge Street at the west end of Camp Street, a
fully restored brick building where gunpowder was cached for
goldfield blasting in the 1850s. Both are open 10 a.m. to 4:30
p.m. daily from Boxing Day (Dec. 26) to May 31, then Sundays
and holidays only the rest of the year.

Other buildings of special interest include the **H.M. Training
Prison**, the brewery museum in the old **M.B. Cellars** and the
Chinese Burning Towers at Beechworth Cemetery. If time
allows, visit the **Buckland Gallery**, perhaps the most interesting
of several crafts shops in town.

The route south

Milawa is little more than a crossroads on a secondary route
midway between Beechworth and Glenrowan. But it's the site of
one of Australia's finest wineries, the **Brown Brothers
Vineyard and Winery.** John Francis Brown planted the first
vines here in 1889, and four succeeding generations of Browns
have carefully tended them. Sample some of the fermented grape
juice — the Cabernet and Shiraz in red and the Chardonnay and
Frontignac in white are particularly good — and take a bottle or
two along for Melbourne's BYO restaurants.

Glenrowan is 21 km (13 miles) due west. Here, in 1880, an
infamous 25-year-old outlaw named Ned Kelly and his three-man
gang were cornered by police at the Glenrowan Inn. Kelly's
companions, including his brother, were killed in a shoot-out;
Ned himself was wounded and brought to trial in Melbourne,
were he was hanged.

Over a period of fewer than three years before his capture,
Kelly had cemented a reputation as a larcenous murderer. Yet his
exploits — he was a superb horseman who wore a 97-pound hand-
moulded suit of armour to protect himself — so fascinated
Australians of past and present that he has been immortalised in
poems, plays, paintings and even a film starring Mick Jagger.

You can't miss Glenrowan's Kelly kitsch, even if you want to.
A Paul Bunyan-esque statue of Ned himself, garbed in his armour
and sporting a rifle, holds up a train emerging from a tunnel
beside the Hume Highway. The so-called Glenrowan Tourist
Centre contains the Ned Kelly Sound and Visual Museum, with a
fully animated gunfight half-hourly from 10 a.m. to 4 p.m. daily
(admission A$5 (£2.40)); next door is a recreation of the cabin

that Ned and his family called home; and everywhere you look there are Kelly T-shirts, books, records, cassette tapes, mugs, keychains, pennants and everything else imaginable. I can only advise you to keep your pennies in your pocket when you stop.

If you stop for groceries another 24 km (15 miles) down the road at **Benalla,** famous for its rose gardens from late October to March, you can take your picnic basket to **Lake Nillahcootie,** an oasis at the foot of Mount Samaria some 40 km (25 miles) south of town via the Midland Highway. After lunch, bypass Mansfield and pick up the Maroondah Highway, crossing the northern arm of serpentine Lake Eildon and continuing to charming Alexandra, the majestic Cathedral Range, and magnificent Maroondah fern forest. You'll arrive at the town of **Healesville** about 175 km (109 miles) from your picnic stop.

But don't stop in town. Follow the signs another 5 km southeast to the **Sir Colin McKenzie Wildlife Sanctuary,** often known simply as the 'Healesville Sanctuary'. This 79-acre reserve is home to nearly 2,000 mammals, birds and reptiles of 200 species, all of them Australian natives. Few are behind bars, and visitors have the opportunity to stroll freely through kangaroo enclosures and parrot aviaries. You'll find everything from koalas to platypuses, wombats to Tasmanian devils, emus to lyrebirds. The sanctuary is open 9 a.m. to 5 p.m. every day of the year (arrive before 3.30 if you want to see the platypus); admission is reasonable at A$5 (£2.40). A restaurant and gift shop are on the

grounds. I consider the sanctuary — established in 1921 in this
natural bushland setting — to be Australia's best wildlife park.
Others apparently agree, for it is the most visited attraction in the
state of Victoria.

If you stay at the sanctuary until the closing hour, you'll avoid
most of the rush-hour traffic (it will be coming toward you,
instead of with you) as you drive the final 62 km (40 miles) west
to Melbourne. Just stay on the Maroondah Highway all the way
into the city.

Melbourne orientation

A stately and sophisticated metropolis of 2.9 million people,
Melbourne (pronounced 'Melb'n', not 'Mel-born') is Australia's
second city. Its elegant Victorian buildings and large
Mediterranean and Asian population combine to give it a
cosmopolitan Old World atmosphere. It's no accident that
Melbourne is the shopping, dining, entertainment and sporting
capital of the country.

Melbourne's role as Australia's financial centre had more
practical roots. Never a penal settlement, it was founded in 1835
by Europeans seeking to escape the more restrictive conditions on
Tasmania. When the Victorian goldfields boomed in the 1850s,
Melbourne became the centre through which the riches were
shipped. With their newfound wealth, Melbournians endowed
their city with broad boulevards, beautiful parks and classically
handsome architecture. And although Sydney, with its superior
harbour and 50-year head start, was the country's best-known
city, it was Melbourne that became Australia's first national
capital (1901-1927) and the host of its only Olympic Games
(1956).

With a latitude of 38 degrees south, about the same distance
from the Equator as Malaga in Spain is north, Melbourne has
four distinct seasons...sometimes all in one day. Generalisations
can be made — temperatures on summer days often reach the 80s
Fahrenheit, while winter days average in the mid 50s — but the
weather is definitely fickle, especially in the autumn months.

Melbourne's core is a neatly planned 1-by-2 km grid on the
north bank of the Yarra River, with nine parallel streets running
north–south and an equal number (five main streets and four
widened alleys) crossing them from east to west. Swanston Street,
which continues south across the Yarra, and Elizabeth Street,
which connects to the Sydney–Canberra and Ballarat–Adelaide
roads, are the main north–south thoroughfares. They are
intersected by Flinders Street, flanking the river and the main
metropolitan railway station; Collins Street, the address of most
banks; Bourke Street, known for its shopping west of Swanston

Street and its Chinatown east; Lonsdale Street, part of it called
The Greek Precinct; and LaTrobe Street, which extends east via
Victoria Parade toward Healesville and the Dandenongs. You'll
enter the city by this latter route.

City transport

The Metropolitan Transit System, known as the Met (tel.
617-0900), comprising rail and tram services, is Australia's best
public transport network. The trains stop at 235 stations within
about a 40-km (25-mile) radius of the city centre, and the web of
electric trams (the only ones in Australia) fill in the gaps that the
trains neglect. It seems as though you're never more than a
couple of streets away from one. The system runs from 5:20 a.m.
to 12:30 a.m. Monday to Saturday, 6:35 a.m. to 11:45 p.m. on
Sunday. Single-ride tickets within the 'Inner Neighbourhood' —
which includes almost all tourist attractions of note — are 70
cents (33p); an unlimited travel two-hour ticket is $1.20 (60p);
and an all-day ticket is $2.30 (£1.10). You can buy these and other
tickets, as well as get free maps and more complete transit
information, at Met depots, railway stations and the Royal Arcade
kiosk between Bourke and Little Collins Streets.

A new and integral part of the Met is the Melbourne
Underground Rail Loop, a A$400 million (£190 million) project
linking five stations around the perimeter of the central city.

Melbourne's international and main domestic airport is at
Tullamarine, 19 km (12 miles) northwest of the city centre. It is
served by taxis and by special buses with direct connections to
downtown hotels.

Where to stay

At the top of the line, Melbourne has two outstanding hotels
which eschew modern steel and concrete for the classic look:
Menzies at Rialto, 459 Collins Street (tel. 62-0111), and **The
Windsor,** 103 Spring Street (tel. 63-0261). The Menzies has
created an atrium out of two neo-Gothic 19th century buildings,
while The Windsor, opposite the old Parliament House, has
retained its century-old feeling right down to the stained-glass
dome lights in the dining room. Both cost A$110 (£52) and up.

At the top of the moderate price bracket, I like the centrally-
located **Hotel Australia,** 266 Collins Street (tel. 653-0401),
which still feels like it must have when it was US Gen. Jonathan
Wainwright's Second World War headquarters. One columnist
described it as a hotel of 'rescinded greatness'. Its comfortable
rooms go for A$80 (£38) double. But parking is a hassle, so those
with cars might prefer the **Downtowner Motel,** 66 Lygon
Street, Carlton (tel. 347-7733), doubles $53 (£25), close to

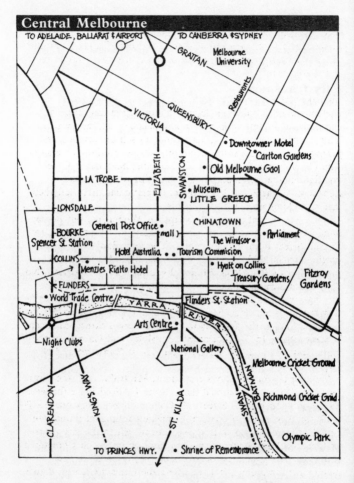

Central Melbourne

TO ADELAIDE, BALLARAT & AIRPORT   TO CANBERRA & SYDNEY

GRATTAN

Melbourne University

QUEENSBURY

VICTORIA

Restaurants

• Downtowner Motel
• Carlton Gardens
• Old Melbourne Gaol

LA TROBE

ELIZABETH

SWANSTON

• Museum
LITTLE GREECE

LONSDALE

CHINATOWN

BOURKE
General Post Office •
(mall)

Spencer St. Station

The Windsor •

• Parliament

Hotel Australia • • Tourism Commission

COLLINS

→ Menzies Rialto Hotel

• Hyatt on Collins

Treasury Gardens

Fitzroy Gardens

← FLINDERS

• World Trade Centre

YARRA

Flinders St. Station

RIVER

Arts Centre •

— Night Clubs

National Gallery •

Melbourne Cricket Ground

BATMAN

SWAN

Richmond Cricket Grnd

CLARENDON

KING'S WAY

ST. KILDA

Olympic Park

TO PRINCES HWY.   • Shrine of Remembrance

Melbourne's best restaurant strip; or in East Melbourne, the
Albert Heights Apartments, 83 Albert Street, with one-
bedroom kitchen suites for $68 (£32).

In the economy class, try the **Victoria Hotel,** 215 Little
Collins Street (tel. 63-0441), in the centre; or the charming
Magnolia Court, 101 Powlett Street, East Melbourne (tel.
417-2782), facing Fitzroy Gardens. For budget lodging, the city's
two **YHA youth hostels** are within a street of each other in
North Melbourne, 3 km from the centre. The larger of the two,
76 Chapman Street, (tel. 328-3595), charges A$7.50 (£3.60) a
head for its 50 double rooms. The older dormitory-style hostel at

500 Abbotsford Street (tel. 328-2880) charges $8 (£3.80). You can
also find good accommodation all year round at the University of
Melbourne's **International House,** 241 Royal Parade, Parkville
(tel. 347-2351), about 4 km north of the centre, with single rooms
and shared baths.

Where to eat

Melbourne is an epicure's delight, a city with a multitude of
excellent restaurants to appeal to any palate. . .and any wallet.
This is partly a response to its attitude of self-importance, but
perhaps even more a result of its broad base of ethnic diversity.
The Greeks (only Athens and Thessalonika have larger Greek
populations than Melbourne), Italians, Yugoslavs, Turks,
Lebanese, Chinese and Vietnamese, in particular, have left their
marks on Melbourne's dining habits.

There are several restaurant 'strips' in Melbourne, but perhaps
none so acclaimed as Lygon Street in Carlton, a short stroll up
Russell Street from the city centre. The main Italian
neighbourhood of Melbourne, this is the place for pasta and
pizzas. **Toto's** (No. 101), **El Gambero** (No. 215), **Il Gusto** (No.
256) and **Tiamo's** (No. 303) are among the best known, all
serving good meals for less than A$10 (£4.75) per person. But
this district is no longer strictly Italian; check the side streets for
Japanese food at the **Samurai,** 210 Drummond Street; Mexican
at **Cha Chi's,** 161 Nicholson Street; Malay and Chinese at the
Bali House, 157 Elgin Street; vegetarian at **Shakahari,** 329
Lygon Street.

Melbourne's most famous restaurant, **Mietta's,** is in the centre
near the deluxe international hotels — at 7 Alfred Place (between
Exhibition and Russell Streets off Collins Street). Fork out A$100
(£48) for two, and you'll get an exquisite continental dinner with
equally generous service. But you can eat well in the city centre
without breaking your budget. You can't go wrong in Chinatown
(Little Bourke Street east of Swanston) if you check out the
menus in the windows and see where the locals are eating. I like
the **Bamboo House,** 47 Little Bourke Street, for Mandarin
cuisine and the **Empress of China,** 120 Little Bourke Street, for
Cantonese.

The Greek restaurants on Lonsdale Street east of Swanston are
also excellent. Try **Stalactites** (open 24 hours) at Lonsdale and
Russell Streets. You'll find even more Greek eateries — plus
plenty of Vietnamese places — in the Richmond district east of
the city centre. Similarly, there's a Turkish dining strip on
Sydney Road in Brunswick, north of the centre.

A personal favourite for a binge is **Percy's,** 384 Punt Road,
South Yarra, an innovative BYO spot with a blackboard menu

that changes daily. Other local choices include **Cafe Lisboa**
(Portuguese), 413 Brunswick Street, Fitzroy; **Costa Brava**
(Spanish), 36 Johnston Street, Fitzroy; and **Isabella's,** a bistro at
Russell and Little Collins Streets in the centre.

For lunch, **Jimmy Watson's Wine Bar,** 333 Lygon Street, is
hard to beat for good, cheap cuisine in an amiable atmosphere.
On the south side, the **Station Hotel,** Chapel and Peel Streets in
Prahran, has counter meals for as little as A\$3 (£1.40).

With some 2,000 restaurants in Melbourne, there's never a fear
about where to eat. So sophisticated is the city in its dining
habits, there's a white-linen restaurant aboard a tram, and another
on a double-decker bus!

Helpful hints

The **Victorian Tourism Centre** (tel. 602-9444), known as
'Victour', handles tourist information on Melbourne city as well
as Victoria. It is centrally located at 230 Collins Street and is
open 9 a.m. to 5 p.m. Monday to Friday, 9 a.m. to noon
Saturday. There is also a **Melbourne Tourism Authority** (tel.
654-2288) on the 20th floor of Nauru House, 80 Collins Street.

The **General Post Office,** at the corner of Bourke and
Elizabeth Streets, is open 8 a.m. to 6 p.m. Monday to Friday.
Most city banks are open 9:30 a.m. to 4 p.m. Monday to
Thursday, 9:30 a.m. to 5 p.m. Friday. Shop hours vary, but you
can generally expect shops in the centre to be open from 9 a.m.
to 5:30 p.m. Monday to Thursday, 9 a.m. to 9 p.m. Friday, 9
a.m. to noon Saturday.

In case of emergencies, dial 000.

TOUR 8

MELBOURNE

Explore the city today. Wander through ethnic neighbourhoods, sophisticated shopping arcades, the high-brow banking district. The Old Gaol and the National Museum of Victoria are worthwhile stops. Don't miss the beautiful Victorian Arts Centre or the nation's best botanic gardens. But don't overdo the sightseeing. Here in sports-crazy Melbourne, try to soak up some local culture by attending (depending on the season) a 'footie' (Australian rules football) match, cricket test or horse race.

Suggested schedule

9:00	A good way to see Melbourne is to start at the north end of the city centre and work your way south on Swanston Street. First stop is Victoria Market, where rows of fresh fruit vendors can supply a juicy breakfast.
10:00	The Old Melbourne Gaol and Penal Museum.
10:45	The National Museum of Victoria, last resting place of Phar Lap.
11:45	Explore the Greek Precinct and Chinatown, stopping in one or the other for lunch.
1:00	Bourke Street Mall and shopping arcades.
2:00	Collins Street, Melbourne's true 'Golden Mile'.
2:30	Victorian Arts Centre, the largest multi-arts complex in the world.
3:30	The National Gallery of Victoria, Australia's finest art museum.
5:00	Royal Botanic Gardens.
6:00	Dinner.
7:00	Join the fanatic throngs at a sports event. There's always something going on on a Saturday night.
10:00	Climax your day with a little nightlife.

Sightseeing highlights

● **Victoria Market** is a large open-air market near the intersection of Queen and Victoria Streets. (The main entrance is off Franklin Street.) On Tuesday, Friday and Saturday mornings starting at 6:00 a.m., it's a multicultural potpourri of fruit and vegetable vendors, while on Sundays from 9:00 a.m. to 4:00 p.m., it turns into an enormous flea market especially popular among craft and antique dealers.

● ●**The Old Melbourne Gaol and Penal Museum,** Russell Street neat Lygon, is a dank and morbid but fascinating relic of the days (1841 to 1929) when men were men and felons were hanged. Here are the gallows and isolation cells known and feared by hundreds of convicts, including the notorious bushranger Ned Kelly. The gaol exhibits Kelly's handmade armour and his 'death mask', created for phrenologists to study possible clues to his deviant behaviour. Open 10:00 a.m. to 5:00 p.m. daily except Sunday. Admission A$3 (£1.40).

● ●**The National Museum of Victoria,** Swanston and LaTrobe Streets, has an excellent exhibition of state history, a new science and technology section, plus good natural history and ethnography displays. Deep within its chambers, however, is the reason so many Australians consider this a religious site. Phar Lap, generally regarded as the greatest racehorse that ever lived, stands within a glass display case — at least, his stuffed skin does. (His heart is in Canberra.) The steed won an incredible 37 of his 51 starts, earning over A$133,000 (£63,300) before dying a mysterious death in Menlo Park, California, in 1932 at the age of 5H. (If you saw the 1983 Australian film, you know all this.) The museum is open from 10:00 a.m. to 4:45 p.m. Monday to Saturday, 2:00 to 4:45 p.m. Sunday. Free admission.

The Greek Precinct on Lonsdale Street, from Swanston to Russell Street, is being upgraded to emphasise the outdoor cafés and colourful specialist shops. The traditional Edwardian character of the buildings has been maintained. If you're here in March or April, chances are you'll catch a festival.

●**Chinatown** — two blocks from Swanston Street to Exhibition Street, bisected by Little Bourke Street — is linked to the Greek Precinct via Heffernan Lane. Chinese have lived in this neighbourhood since 1854. The opium dens have long since closed, but many of the butchers, bakers and candlemakers still ply trades learned from their forefathers. Today, the restaurants and shops on Little Bourke and its side lanes, especially Celestial Avenue, comprise the most interesting Chinatown in the Southern Hemisphere. The Museum of Chinese Australian History, 22 Cohen Place, contains photographs, artifacts, and an audio-visual presentation. Open weekdays except Tuesday 10:00 a.m. to 4:30 p.m., weekends noon to 4:30 p.m.

●**Bourke Street Mall** is the shopping centre of Australia's shopping capital. The Myer Emporium, for example, is the world's second largest department store (after Marshall Field's in Chicago), taking up a good portion of two city blocks on the north side of the mall. The south side of the mall is interlaced by a maze of delightfully restored shopping arcades. In particular, check out the Royal Arcade, with its outrageous 1892 clock depicting Gog and Magog striking the time.

There are several other great shopping streets in the suburbs. Armadale High Street is packed with antique, craft, books and clothing shops; Chapel Street and Toorak Road are the hubs of a glitzy high-fashion neighbourhood in South Yarra; and St Kilda's Acland Street is famous for its pastry shops.

Parliament House, on Spring Street at the east end of Bourke Street, was built in 1856 and served as the federal Parliament until the provisional house in Canberra opened in 1927. It still serves as Victoria's state assembly chambers. Guided tours are offered at 10:00 a.m., 11:00 a.m., and 2:00 p.m. Monday through Friday.

● **Collins Street** is where the nation's most important financial institutions are housed, many of them in Victorian gold-rush masterpieces spliced between steel-and-glass skyscrapers. If you're here on a weekday, take a walking tour, starting at the ANZ Banking Museum (open 9:30 a.m. to 4:00 p.m. Monday to Friday) in the basement of the Australia-New Zealand Bank, 386 Collins Street. Then step inside the institution upstairs for a look-around, and also have a peek into the Bank of New Zealand (No. 395), National Australian Bank (No. 335) and Westpac (No. 331). The Melbourne Stock Exchange, 351 Collins Street, has a third floor visitors gallery with a broad view of the trading floor. It's open Monday to Friday from 9:00 a.m. to noon and 2:00 to 5:00 p.m.

● ● **The Victorian Arts Centre** is modern Melbourne's pride and joy. The city proudly trumpets that this is 'the largest arts centre in the world'. Indeed, the complex — completed only in 1985 — includes a 2,600-seat concert hall, three theatres for opera, ballet and drama, three licensed restaurants, an art shop, a museum, and the adjoining National Gallery of Victoria. Its 500-foot Eiffel-like spire, which towers over the Yarra River beside St Kilda Road, can be seen for miles around.

A variety of tours are offered to show off the Centre and its unusual architecture. There are morning tea tours weekdays for A$10 (£4.75), or luncheon tours for A$18 (£8.60). Evening tours, starting promptly at 5:00 p.m. Monday to Friday, include dinner and a show for A$45 (£21.40). Short tours at 10:30 a.m. daily cost A$2.75 (£1.30); Sunday backstage tours are A$6 (£2.85).

The Melbourne Symphony Orchestra often plays free lunch-time concerts, and every Friday from 5:00 to 7:00 p.m., there's a free jazz show in the basement Monsanto Lounge. Bookings should be made for all other performances and tours by calling 617-8211.

●**The Performing Arts Museum,** in the concert hall, is highly
regarded internationally. Its changing exhibits range from silent
films or horror films to recreations of Dame Nellie Melba's
operatic recordings. Open 11:00 a.m. to 5:00 p.m. Monday to
Friday, noon to 5:00 p.m. Saturday. Admission A$1.10 (50p).

● ● ●**The National Gallery of Victoria,** on the south side of
the Victorian Arts Centre at 180 St Kilda Road, was Australia's
first public art gallery (founded in 1861) and is still the finest in
the Southern Hemisphere. Its most popular galleries to overseas
visitors are those of Aboriginal and Oceanic art and of Australian
art, especially featuring its noted Heidelberg school of late 19th
century impressionists — Tom Roberts, Arthur Streeton,
Frederick McCubbin and Charles Condon. Its collection of more
than 50,000 works also includes divisions of European, British
and American art, Asian art, pre-Columbian art, costumes and
textiles, decorative arts, prints and drawings, and photography.
Open daily except Monday from 10:00 a.m. to 5:00 p.m.
Admission A$1.20 (60p).

● ●**The Royal Botanic Gardens,** a half-kilometre stroll south
and east of the Arts Centre, are considered one of the world's
best landscaped gardens. More than 12,000 plant species thrive in
the 88 acres of lawns, garden beds and ornamental lakes, along
with over 50 species of birds.

Adjacent to the gardens is the much larger **King's Domain,**
containing the massive Shrine of Remembrance war memorial; the
circa-1840 LaTrobe's Cottage, Victoria's original government
house (open daily 10:00 a.m. to 4:30 p.m., admission A$1.60
(75p)); and the Sidney Myer Music Bowl, an outdoor
amphitheatre in the summer, a covered public ice rink in the
winter. The 11-km Yarra River Bikeway starts here; bicycles can
be hired opposite the Botanic Gardens in Alexandra Avenue from
11:00 a.m. to dusk weekends and holidays.

Melbourne's other famous parks include **Fitzroy Gardens,** in
East Melbourne between Wellington Parade and Albert Street. Its
highlight is Captain Cook's Cottage, transported here from
Yorkshire in 1934 and reassembled (open 9:00 a.m. to 5:00 p.m.
daily, admission 80 cents (38p)). The adjacent **Treasury
Gardens,** facing Spring Street, contain a John Kennedy
memorial. **Carlton Gardens,** Victoria Street opposite Spring
Street, contain the Royal Exhibition Buildings built in 1880 for
the inauguration of the commonwealth of Australia. **Albert Park,**
between South Melbourne and St Kilda, has a large lake with
boats for hire.

●**The Royal Melbourne Zoo,** on Elliott Avenue in Royal Park
(north of the city centre), is the third oldest zoo on earth. The
aviary, they say, is bigger than Paris' Cathedral of Notre Dame.

The 55 acres have recently been relandscaped, with most of the 336 species now in simulated natural environments. Open 1:00 p.m. to 5:30 p.m. daily. Admission A$4.40 (£2.10).

● **Como House** (1855), on Como Avenue in South Yarra, and **Ripponlea** (1887), on Hotham Street in Elsternwick, are two beautiful colonial mansions set in spacious suburban gardens. Both have been refurnished with the trappings of the Victorian élite; both are open daily 10:00 a.m. to 5:00 p.m. and charge A$3.50 (£1.66) admission. (Ripponlea has limited winter hours.)

● **The Polly Woodside,** anchored in the Yarra River at Normanby Road and Phayer Street in South Melbourne, is a restored iron-hulled Irish sailing vessel now finding new duty as the focus of a maritime museum. Open Monday to Friday, 10.00 a.m. to 4:00 p.m., and weekends noon to 5:00 p.m. Admission A$4 (£1.90).

The City Explorer Bus (tel. 598-5355) leaves the Flinders Street Station hourly from 10:00 a.m. to 4:00 p.m. every day but Monday. It stops at Captain Cook's Cottage, the Old Gaol, the National Museum, the Polly Woodside and the National Gallery. One-day tickets for the on-again, off-again loop are A$5 (£2.40).

Sports in Melbourne

Australia in general, and Melbourne in particular, comes to a stop on the first Tuesday of November when the Melbourne Cup is run at Flemington Racecourse. In fact, this world-famous horse race is celebrated as a public holiday in Victoria. And that's indicative of the reverence with which Melbournians regard sports in general.

After all, this is where Australian Rules Football was invented. Victorians have set out to evangelise the world with this sport that isn't soccer, isn't rugby, certainly isn't American football, but has elements of all three — and some of its own. Most of Australia's capital cities are now represented in the Victorian Football League, and games are often televised in the UK on Channel 4. Upwards of 100,000 fans attend major matches at the venerable Melbourne Cricket Ground (MCG). The season starts in April and concludes with the Grand Final on the last Saturday of September.

About the time 'footie' is winding down, cricket is just beginning. Its season runs from October to March, concluding with the Sheffield Shield, pitting each Australian state against the others until one claims the national championship.

Melbourne hosts many other important sports events, including a major international tennis tournament. To find out what's happening (and where) during your visit, check the sports page of *The Age*, Australia's best newspaper.

Melbourne nightlife

Melbourne doesn't have any equivalent to Sydney's Kings Cross.
Its nightlife is spread across the metropolis, from the city centre
to the suburbs. St Kilda, a short hop south of the city centre,
tends to be the most 'in' area; Richmond (east) and Carlton
(north) can also be lively.

The Friday morning edition of *The Age* gives full listings of the
entertainment week ahead. Rock music dominates the scene, but
you'll find far more jazz and acoustic music in Melbourne than in
other big cities.

The only thing approaching a central 'strip' is King Street from
Collins to Flinders Streets. In one block, there's live rock at
Inflation and the **Melbourne Underground;** discos at the
Hippodrome and the **York Butter Factory;** cabaret at **Lazars
International;** jazz and folk at the **Grainstore Tavern.** Some
of the nightspots are open all night — you can 'rage' 'til 7:00
a.m.

The **Limerick Arms Hotel** in South Melbourne and the
Bridge Hotel in Richmond are two of the city's best venues for
live jazz, while the **Moomba Hotel** in North Melbourne is good
for country sounds Wednesday to Friday.

The No. 1 meeting spot in town, at the time of writing, was
the new **Hyatt on Collins,** at the corner of Russell Street. The
casual bars and restaurants in the basement of its atrium are
packed from the off-work hours to closing. **Zanie's,** a trendy bar-
bistro at Lonsdale and Russell Streets, draws a good crowd. The
Sherlock Holmes Inn, 421 Collins Street, attracts lovers of
traditional British pubs.

Young and Jackson's, 1 Swanston Street at Flinders, is
Melbourne's most famous pub and one of its oldest. Since the
Melbourne Exhibition of 1880, it has displayed above its bar an
oil painting of 'Chloe' — a full-length nude that once shocked
Victorian sentiments.

For symphony, theatre, opera, ballet, etc., the obvious first
choice is the **Victorian Arts Centre** (see 'Sightseeing highlights').
Other major stages in the centre — **Her Majesty's Theatre,** 219
Exhibition Street, and the **Princess Theatre,** 163 Spring Street
— are within three streets of each other. This section of central
Melbourne, along Bourke Street between Spring and Swanston, is
also the location of most cinema houses for first-run films.

Melbourne hosts two major festivals during the year. Moomba,
in March, is the Mardi Gras Down Under. Gian Carlo Menotti's
Spoleto Arts Festival, in September/October, is a more sedate but
culturally fulfilling event.

TOUR 9

BALLARAT

Ballarat is synonymous with two subjects near and dear to
Australians' hearts: gold and independence. This tour covers both
ends of this historic Victorian city — Sovereign Hill, the
country's No. 1 theme park, faithful to its 1850 heyday; and the
Eureka Stockade, site (in 1854) of a much-heralded rebellion
unique in Australian history.

Suggested schedule

8.00	Leave Melbourne, heading west on the Great Western Freeway (Highway 8).
10:00	Arrive in Ballarat. Sovereign Hill is the town's central attraction. Plan to spend several hours, including lunch.
2:00	Cross the street to the Gold Museum.
3:00	Relive the glory of the Eureka Stockade.
4:00	See Montrose Cottage, the Botanic Gardens or another of Ballarat's attractions.
5:30	Head back to Melbourne for dinner and rest.

Ballarat orientation

Victoria's second largest city with a population of 90,000, Ballarat
is located 113 km (70 miles) west of Melbourne. It was founded
by gold diggers in 1851 and quickly became an Eldorado, with
fortune hunters from around the world converging on the
settlement after hearing fairy tales about gold nuggets being
plucked off the streets. In fact, the argonauts had to work for
their gold, but they pulled an estimated 20 million ounces from
the hills before the last mine closed in 1918. At today's prices,
that would be worth about £5.7 billion.

Much of the money that gold wrought was poured into
constructing a beautiful town on the frontier. With the opening of
the railroad in 1862, Ballarat became the gateway to western
Victoria, and its future was assured. Today it is known for its
gardens and art galleries as much as for its historic sites.

The Western Highway — Stuart Street through most of the
centre — bisects Ballarat into northern and southern halves. The
Gold Centre Tourist Centre (tel. 053/32-2694), on Lydiard Street
outside the railway station, is two blocks north of the highway
near the business centre of town. Sovereign Hill is perhaps a mile
south of the centre on Bradshaw Street (just off Main Road). The

Eureka Stockade, exhibition and diorama are on Stawell Street,
just south of the Western Highway at the east end of Ballarat.

City transport

If you don't drive to Ballarat — if your perchance take the train
or bus from Melbourne — you can shuttle to the town's
attractions on the Shutttlebus (tel. 31-2655). Seven loop trips a
day are operated around the city, taking in Sovereign Hill and the
Eureka Stockade. You can board between 9:20 a.m. and 4:00 p.m.
at the Tourism Centre at the railway station, disembark and
reboard wherever you choose along the route for A$8 (£3.80).
The Shuttlebus also travels between Ballarat and Melbourne's
Tullamarine airport three or four times daily, with A$30 (£14)
covering round-trip transport plus admission charges at Sovereign
Hill and the Eureka Stockade.

Sightseeing highlights

● ● ● Sovereign Hill is a place of living history, an authentic
recreation of Australia's most important gold-mining township of
the 1850s. Operated by a non-profit local association whose 200
volunteers dress in period costume, the park has three main
sections. In the Red Hill Gully Diggings (faithful to the period
1851-1855), brightly dressed miners emerge from their tents and
mud huts to show visitors how to pan for alluvial gold. In the
Goldmining Township (1854-1861), horse-drawn coaches roll past
29 separate working businesses — among them a blacksmith,
coachbuilder, tinsmith, confectioner, printer, potter and furniture
maker with a steam-driven lathe. In the Mining Museum
(1860-1918), you can travel underground to learn how quartz reef
mining was done, while above you a thunderous stamper battery
crushes the gold-bearing quartz.

Main Street is Sovereign Hill's core. You can dine in style at
the New York Bakery or the licensed United States Hotel. (Take-
away food and barbecue supplies are also available in the
Township.) You can attend comedy sketches in the Victoria
Theatre, or try your hand at skittles in the Empire Bowling
Saloon.

Low-cost accommodation is available at Government Camp, a
recreated 1850s military barracks on a hill overlooking the
Township. Though the buildings might appear old, they're
comfortably modern within. Families of four can stay for A$35
(£16.50) a night (for four); there's also a YHA youth hostel on the
site.

The park is open daily (except Christmas) from 9:30 a.m. to
5:00 p.m. Admission is A$8 (£3.80); for A$10 (£4.75), you can
get a Gold Pass which includes a coach ride and admission to the

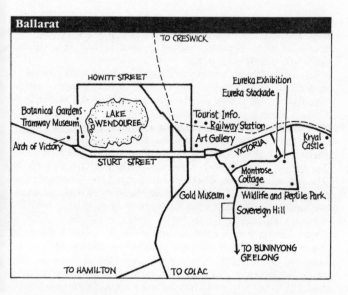

Ballarat

adjacent Gold Museum.

● ●**The Gold Museum,** on Bradshaw Street across from the Sovereign Hill car park, is a worthy adjunct to the theme park. Its historical exhibits, while emphasising the gold rush era and Eureka Stockade rebellion, also recall central Victoria's Aboriginal history and the creation of its wool industry. The Gold Pavilion displays important private collections of rare gold coins from around the world and turn-of-the-century Chinese artifacts. Open 9:30 a.m. to 5:30 p.m. daily except Christmas. Admission A$1.50 (70p).

● ●**Eureka Stockade** is a name with the same ring to Australians as the Alamo has to Texans. Like Davy Crockett, Jim Bowie *et al.,* the miners lost this battle — but they won the war.

Mercilessly taxed and oppressed by the British colonial administration, the diggers made a gallant stand for their democratic rights. The climax came on 3 December 1854, when government troopers attacked a stockaded position held by miners near the Eureka diggings. Six troopers and 22 miners died. The tragedy shocked Victoria's colonial leaders into introducing long-awaited reforms in the goldfields. Within a year, two leaders of the revolt were elected to the first Victorian Parliament under a new constitution.

Today, at the Eureka Street Parklands (at the corner of Stawell Street), the rebellion is remembered by a memorial, a reconstructed stockade and a diorama of the incident. More impressive is the Eureka Exhibition, diagonally from the memorial at Eureka and Kline Streets, with a series of computer-controlled scenes depicting various episodes of the revolt. Open daily 9:00 a.m. to 6:00 p.m.

The miners' famous Southern Cross banner flew over the stockade for only five days — yet Aussies hold it in high esteem. The Eureka flag can be seen in the Ballarat Fine Art Gallery, 40 Lydiard Street (near the Tourism Centre).

● **Montrose Cottage,** 111 Eureka Street, is the last original blue-stone masonry cottage surviving from 1850s Ballarat. Classified by the National Trust, it contains the small Eureka Museum of Social History. Open daily 9:30 a.m. to 5:30 p.m.

The 100-acre **Botanic Gardens** encompass Lake Wendouree on the northwest side of Ballarat. Prime Ministers Avenue, within the gardens, is flanked by bronze busts of all Australian prime ministers, right up to the leader in 1989, Bob Hawke.

Kryal Castle, 8 km east of Ballarat on the Western Highway, is a curiosity: a recreated medieval castle where costumed actors re-enact the life and pageantry of the Middle Ages. There's jousting, sword-fighting, even the occasional hanging, and a tavern where a medieval banquet is held every Saturday night. Open 9:30 a.m. to 5:30 p.m. daily except Christmas.

Golda's World of Dolls, 148 Eureka Street, displays more than 2,000 rare, antique and period-costumed dolls from all over the world. Open 1:00 to 5:00 p.m. Monday to Thursday, 10:00 a.m. to 5:00 p.m. weekends and holidays. Closed Fridays.

The Arch of Victory, at the west end of Ballarat marks the beginning of the tree-lined, 21 km-long Avenue of Honour to the men and women of Ballarat who volunteered for active service abroad during World War One.

TOUR 10

DANDENONG RANGES AND PHILLIP ISLAND

The 'Blue Dandenongs', a relaxing day trip on the east side of Melbourne, contain many beautiful gardens, a unique sculpture forest, a park noted for its lyrebirds, and various other attractions. The day's highlight comes at dusk, when hundreds and thousands of tiny fairy penguins parade from the sea to their burrows up a concrete walkway as hundreds of flash cameras click away.

Suggested schedule

9:00	Leave Melbourne as soon as rush hour has ended.
10:15	Stroll through the William Ricketts Sanctuary, with its environmentally orientated sculptures of Aboriginal Mother Nature theme.
11:00	Visit Mount Dandenong Observatory to gaze at the high-rises of Melbourne in the distance.
11:30	The pretty artisans' village of Olinda is also the site of the National Rhododendron Gardens.
12:15	Lunchtime at a tearoom in Olinda or Sassafras.
1:00	The elusive lyrebird runs free in Sherbrooke Forest Park.
2:00	Take a quick swim at Emerald Lake Park or visit a model railway museum near the terminus of the Puffing Billy steam train from Belgrave.
4:30	Arrive at Phillip Island for the penguin parade. The parade occurs about dusk, so the exact time varies from season to season.
After dark	Return to Melbourne, stopping for dinner en route.

(*Note:* On Sundays, these roads are always packed by local day-trippers. Plan to skip a couple of attractions in the Dandenongs to reach Phillip Island on time.)

The Dandenong Ranges

The forested mountains east of Melbourne aren't especially high — Mount Dandenong itself is only 633 metres (2,076 feet) — but that's enough to lift them above the occasional smog of

Port Phillip Bay and endow them with a rich plant and animal
life. A surprising number of artists and nature lovers choose to
live in the Dandenongs and commute 60 to 90 minutes (each
way) to the city daily.

The fastest route to the Dandenong Ranges is to head back east
on the Maroondah Highway, as to Healesville, but turn right at
Ringwood on the well-marked Mount Dandenong Road. A drive
of about an hour from the city brings you to Montrose, at the
northern end of the Mount Dandenong Tourist Road. Sightseeing
highlights of the Dandenongs, moving down the road from north
to south, include:

● ● **William Ricketts Sanctuary.** Like J.R.R. Tolkien gone
mad, Ricketts — who celebrated his 89th birthday in 1988 — is an
eccentric musician-turned-artist-turned environmental radical. His
enchanting clay sculptures decorate a lovely fern forest on the
slopes of Mount Dandenong; indeed, they are a part of the forest,
carefully moulded to existing trees, rocks and brooks. All of
Ricketts' work has Aboriginal and spiritual over-tones. His more
recent sculptures also make fierce animal rights and anti-
exploitation statements. 'Being part of nature,' he writes, 'we are
brothers to the birds and trees. Will you then join us in the
sacredness of beauty?' Open 10:00 a.m. to 5:00 p.m. daily.
Admission A$2.50 (£1.20).

● **Mount Dandenong Observatory.** Outside the mountain-top
restaurant and tea room are a roadside observation area and a
handful of coin-in-the-slot telescopes to gaze across at the
metropolis of Melbourne in the near west.

Edward Henty Cottage. A pioneer museum and antique shop
occupy the former home of one of the Dandenongs' early
residents. Located a short distance above Olinda. Admission to
the museum is A$1.50 (70p).

● **Olinda.** Art galleries and small restaurants specialising in
midday Devonshire teas line the road around this picturesque
village. It's worth getting out of the car and walking around.

● **National Rhododendron Gardens.** Rhody lovers go bananas
over these Olinda gardens in the spring and summer. By autumn,
there's not much to look at. Admission A$3 (1.40).

● **Sherbrooke Forest Park.** Take any of the tranquil trails
through this lush nature preserve and you're likely to see or hear
the lyrebird, a grouse-sized ground bird with a long, lacy,
peacock-like tail used in courtship demonstrations. The lyrebird
is remarkable for its ability to mimic almost any sound it hears,
from other birds to machinery. (I was once awakened while
camping by the sound of a logging truck. There were no logging
roads nearby, but there were lyrebirds.) Also in the forest are
Sherbrooke Falls, Alfred Nicholas Memorial Gardens and four

picnic grounds with barbecue facilities.

Fern Tree Gully National Park. Just above the town of Upper
Ferntree Gully, this small park encompassing a valley of beautiful
fern trees offers pleasant walks and colourful rosellas galore.

Belgrave. Another artists' community, somewhat larger than
Olinda, Belgrave lies at a major junction in the Dandenongs. It's
best known as the depot for Puffing Billy.

● ● **Puffing Billy.** Australia's best-known narrow-gauge steam
railroad — built in 1900 to carry farm produce — packs its wooden
cars with weekend and holiday day-trippers year-round, daily
during school holidays (except on days of total fire ban). Puffing
Billy typically leaves Belgrave at 10:30 a.m. on its 13-km (8-mile),
40-minute run up and down the ridges to Emerald Lake Park,
returning at 12:40 p.m. There are additional runs on weekends.
The round-trip fare is A$8.20 (£3.90) for adults, A$5.50 (£2.60)
for kids. (Call 870-8411 for timetable specifics.) There's a Steam
Museum at Menzies Creek, open 11:00 a.m. to 5:00 p.m.
Sundays and holidays, with a collection of early locomotives. You
may not have time for a ride on Puffing Billy unless you have an
extra day or two in Melbourne.

● **Emerald Lake Park.** A spacious, well-kept park surrounding
a lake popular with swimmers and fishermen, this is the eastern
terminus of Puffing Billy. Above the station is a pavilion
containing Australia's largest model railway: over 2 kilometres of
track. A youth hostel stands near the park's entrance. In Emerald
village are many quaint shops and craft galleries.

Phillip Island

It will take about 30 minutes to drive from Emerald Lake Park to
Pakenham, and another 90 minutes to follow the South Gippsland
and Bass highways south to San Remo, at the east end of the
604-metre (2,100-foot) Narrows Bridge connecting Phillip Island
to the Victorian mainland.

Phillip Island's main attraction, one of the outstanding sights in
all of Australia, is the **Penguin parade** at Summerland Beach,
near the island's southwestern tip, every night of the year. A
colony of fairy penguins numbering in the thousands spend most
of their days fishing in Bass Strait, returning at dusk to their
burrows in the sand dunes at the protected reserve. Bright lights
illuminate the beach as the penguins straggle in to land and up a
concrete walkway, while a crowd of camera-happy tourists quietly
view from controlled areas behind a wire fence. These little (foot-
high) birds are so cuddly-looking that it's hard not to smile as you
watch them waddle through their nightly ritual, apparently
oblivious to all the human attention.

You can buy tickets to the viewing area (for A$5 (£2.40)) at the

Penguin Reserve office beginning 30 minutes before the parade,
or at the Phillip Island Information Centre near San Remo, open
daily 9:00 a.m. to 5:00 p.m. (Don't tell anyone, but there's
another nightly penguin parade, albeit smaller, off St Kilda
Parade near central Melbourne.)

The penguins aren't the only wild denizens of 25,000-acre
Phillip Island. Koalas roam freely in the eucalyptus groves of
Oswin Roberts Reserve. Fur seals maintain an offshore colony
on **The Nobbies,** a 50 million-year-old volcanic rock stack: up to
4,500 of the marine mammals breed here in November and
December. Mutton birds (short-tailed shearwaters) nest on Cape
Woolamai, the island's southeasternmost point.

Len Leukey Memorial Museum and Gardens at Smith's
Beach, about halfway along the south shore, exhibits a good
collection of vintage cars and racing vehicles from a late-lamented
motor racing track.

The island also features dairy and shell museums, a centre for
wool artisans, three chicory kilns, a historic homestead on
Churchill Island (connected to Phillip Island by a footbridge at
Newhaven), a small zoo, a large blowhole, a cavern, golf courses
and other standard resort amenities.

Cowes, the island's main town (on the north shore), has ample
accommodation and eating places. (In summer, it's best to dine
before the parade, because the restaurants close early.)

TOUR 11

ALICE SPRINGS

Drop your car at Melbourne's Tullamarine Airport and catch a
morning flight to Alice Springs. You'll have all afternoon and
evening to explore this Outback oasis. Visit the Old Telegraph
Station and the Royal Flying Doctor Service. To climax your day,
ride a camel down the dry Todd River bed to dinner at a desert
winery.

Suggested schedule

9:00	Return car to Tullamarine Airport.
10:00	Depart Melbourne on Ansett Flight 77 for Alice Springs.
12:20	Arrive at Alice Springs.
1:00	Check into your accommodation.
1:30	Orientate yourself at the Anzac Hill viewpoint.
1:45	See the Old Telegraph Station.
2:30	Visit the School of the Air.
3:00	Drop in on the Royal Flying Doctor Service.
4:00	Take a camel to dinner.
9:00	Return to Alice Springs.

Leaving Melbourne

Flemington Road leads north into the Calder Highway, taking
you to Melbourne International Airport at Tullamarine. Arrive
well before your flight departure to turn in your hire car.

Ansett Flight 77 operates non-stop to Alice Springs (leaving
Melbourne at 10:00 a.m.) only on Tuesday and Thursdays. On
any other day of the week, you must plan your departure around
7:30 a.m. on either Ansett or Australian Airlines. Both carriers
have daily flights to Alice Springs via Adelaide.

Alice Springs orientation

With a rapidly growing population of about 25,000, 'The Alice' is
the biggest town for more than 800 miles in any direction. A
desert oasis, it is situated in the midst of the MacDonnel Ranges,
almost exactly in the geographic centre of the continent.
Australians call this area 'The Centre' (or 'The Red Centre'
because of the unusual colour of its soil).

Founded in 1872 as a station on the Overland Telegraph Line

between Adelaide and Darwin, it got its name when station master Charles Todd dubbed a permanent waterhole in the bed of the usually dry Todd River 'Alice Springs' after his wife.

When the railroad came through in 1929, the population was still only 200. A road from Adelaide was completed about 1940; only in April 1987 was the final link paved. The population didn't reach 1,000 until the 1950s or 5,000 until the 1970s. Modern tourism, however, has contributed to a boom throughout the Northern Territory, especially in The Alice.

The central business district is a compact 12 square blocks between the highway and the Todd River, bounded by Wills Terrace on the north and Stott Terrace on the south. The Todd Street Mall, recently made a pedestrians-only thoroughfare, stretches for two blocks from Gregory Terrace to Wills Terrace a block west of the river and is regarded as the centre of town. (It is bisected by Parsons Street, and is paralleled to the west by Hartley and Bath Streets and to the east by Leichhardt Terrace overlooking the river.)

The word river, by the way, is a misnomer. To be called a 'local' in Alice Springs, one must have seen the Todd flow its length three times. Some 20-year residents are still waiting to become locals. The river is completely dry most of the year.

The Northern Territory Government Tourist Bureau, 51 Todd St at Parsons St (tel 52-1299), has a wide selection of maps, brochures and other information, including detailed walking and driving tours of the city areas.

City transport

Alice Springs Airport is some 14 km (9 miles) south of the city centre. Pay A$3.50 (£1.66) or A$5 return (£2.40) for shuttle service up the Stuart Highway to the centre.

There's no public transport in Alice Springs except for taxis, and they're rather expensive. If you want to get out and see the town, beyond what you can easily walk to, you have these options:

Hire a car for the day. You can get an open 'moke' for as little as A$17 (£8) a day and 18 cents (8p) a km, plus $5 (£2.40) for insurance. (That's a cost of A$31 (£14.75) if you do 50 km of driving.) A small-sized car will cost around A$25 (£12) a day and 18 cents (8p) a km.

Hire a car and driver, at a rate of A$35 (£16.66) for two hours. The Northern Territory Government Tourist Bureau has a list of operators.

Join a bus tour. Three-hour tours operated by Ansett, AAT King's and CATA Tours, among others, are priced at A$22 (£10.50), including all admissions.

Hire a bicycle or moped. Thrifty Bike Hire on Todd Street has bikes for A$6 (£2.85) an 8-hour day, mopeds for A$20 (£9.50) a day. The tourist bureau can tell you other locations.

Sightseeing highlights

Anzac Hill, named in honour of the combined World War I and II armed forces of Australia and New Zealand, offers a good view of Alice Springs and the surrounding terrain. Drive the circular road off Stuart Highway, or trek up the steep Lions Walk from the end of Bath Street off Wills Terrace.

● ● **The Old Telegraph Station** is 3 km north of Alice Springs off the Stuart Highway. The reserve has restored the original 1872 telegraph station and equipment, and displays early photographs and historical documents. There are nature walks and a small wildlife park nearby, as well as a picnic ground and barbecue area beside the Alice Springs waterhole.

● **The School of the Air** provides education by short-wave radio to children through the Central Australian Outback, some as far as 1,000 km (621 miles) away. Visitors are invited to observe and listen between 1.30 and 3.30 p.m. on school days (Monday to Friday except holidays). The school is located beside Braitling School in Head Street, about 1½ miles north of the centre.

● ● **The Royal Flying Doctor Service** was established in 1939 by the Rev. John Flynn, probably The Alice's best-known historical figure, to deliver medical attention to isolated homesteads by small plane. Today it relies more on radio communication to serve thousands of square miles from New South Wales and Queensland to Western Australia. Tours of the base, near the south end of Bath Street on Stuart Terrace, are offered every half-hour from 9:00 to 11:30 a.m. and 2:00 to 3:30 p.m. Monday to Friday, and from 9:00 to 11:00 a.m. Saturday. Admission is A$1.50 (70p). (Flynn's original aircraft is on display at the Aviation Museum on Memorial Drive, at the old Alice Springs airport.)

● **Panorama Guth,** 65 Hartley Street north of Stott Terrace, is the private gallery of painter Henk Guth, who has created an unusual 360-degree mural of the terrain surrounding Alice Springs. Guth also has a collection of photographs, Aboriginal artifacts and watercolour paintings of the Hermannsburg School. Open 9:00 a.m. to 5:00 p.m. Monday to Friday 9:00 a.m. to noon and 2:00 to 5:00 p.m. Saturday, 2:00 to 5:00 p.m. Sunday. Admission is A$1.50 (70p).

● **Pitchi Richi Sanctuary,** on Aranda Terrace south of Heavitree Gap near the Todd River causeway, combines William Ricketts' unique Aboriginal-theme sculpture with an outdoor folk museum and wild bird refuge. If you missed the Ricketts

Sanctuary in the Dandenong Ranges east of Melbourne, don't
miss this. Open daily 9:00 a.m. to sunset. Admission is A$1.50
(70p).

● **Diorama Village,** 2 km west of the centre of Larapinta
Drive at Bradshaw Drive, uses narrated dioramas to depict
Aboriginal myths — like how the kangaroo got his tail and how the
Milky Way was formed. Open 10:00 a.m. to 5:00 p.m. daily;
admission A$2 (95p).

● Aboriginal art galleries exhibit and sell the arts and crafts of
the native tribes of Central Australia — the Arunta, the Curindji
and the Pitjantjatjara. Browse at the government-operated **Centre
for Aboriginal Artists and Craftsmen,** 86 Todd Street, or any
of a dozen other shops and galleries.

Emily Gap Camel Farm, 4 km south of town on Emily Gap
Road (the Ross Highway), is open for riding these 'ships of the
desert' from 8:00 a.m. to 5:00 p.m. daily. It also has a Magic
Spark Museum of early radio communications. Admission is
A$2.50 (£1.20). **The Mecca Date Garden** on Emily Gap Road
is Australia's only commercial date garden, with 20 varieties of
productive date palms. Open daily 9:30 a.m. to 4:30 p.m.
Admission, including a conducted tour, is A$1.50 (70p).

● **The Henley-on-Todd Regatta** is perhaps the most exciting
boating race never to take place on water. Every year in the last
weekend of August, 40-foot yachts line up in the dry river bed,
gripped tightly on the gunwhale by their crews, who run with
them as fast as they can. It's a good excuse for a party.

Where to stay

The top of the line in Alice Springs is represented by the modern
Sheraton Alice Springs, Barrett Drive (tel. 52-8000), followed
closely by its next-door neighbour, **Lasseter's Casino** (tel.
52-5066). Both are on the south side of town. The **Elkira Motel,**
134 Bath Street (tel. 52-1222); the **Desert Rose Inn,** 15 Railway
Terrace (tel. 52-1411); and the **Oasis Motel,** 10 Gap Road at
Traeger Avenue (tel 52-1444), are centrally located and
moderately priced.

For economy bracket lodging, try the **Arura Safari Lodge,** 18
Warburton Street at Lindsay Avenue (tel. 52-3843). The YWCA's
Stuart Lodge, Stuart Terrace near Todd Street (tel. 52-1894),
takes both men and women. Budget travellers can get a cheap bed
at the **Sandrifter Safari Lodge,** 6 Kharlic Street (tel. 52-8686),
or the **Alice Springs Youth Hostel** at the corner of Todd Street
and Stott Terrace (tel. 52-5016).

Where to eat

Aside from hotel coffee shops and restaurants, there is a good variety of dining establishments in Alice Springs. Steak and spicy food lovers appreciate **Overlanders Steakhouse,** 72 Hartley Street, with meals in the A$8 to A$10 (£3.80 to £4.75) range. Ask for buffalo steak in witchety grub sauce. **The Todd Tavern,** at the corner of the Todd Street Mall and Wills Terrace, has several restaurants, including **The Other Place,** serving counter meals priced from A$4.50 (£2.15) and the more formal **Maxim's** for continental cuisine. **Papa Luigi's Bistro,** at the north end of Todd Street, has pastas, steaks and chicken cacciatore for A$5 (£2.40) and up. **Chopsticks,** in the Ermond Arcade on Hartley Street, is the local Chinese favourite with Cantonese and Szechuan cuisine. Good, cheap breakfasts and lunches cost no more than A$5 (£2.40) at the **Eranova Cafeteria,** 72 Todd Street.

Fifteen km (9½ miles) south of Alice Springs is **Chateau Hornsby,** Central Australia's first and only winery. The wine isn't great, but it's certainly palatable...and dry! There's an informal outdoor barbecue area, fine for lunches, and a pleasant indoor restaurant where local bush balladeer Ted Egan performs most nights. Find it at the end of Petrick Road, off Colonel Rose Drive.

On Sundays, Tuesdays and Fridays, for A$45 (£21.50) you can 'Take a Camel to Dinner' by joining **Frontier Tours'** sundown safari down the Todd River bed to Chateau Hornsby. The price includes an hour on a camel's back and a five-course barramundi (fish) or buffalo roast dinner. The beasts leave Alice Springs at 4:00 p.m. (returning at 9:00 p.m.) October to April and depart at 3:00 p.m. May to September. Book at your hotel or call 53-0444.

Nightlife

Alice Springs isn't Sydney or Melbourne. But it does have a casino. **Lasseter's Casino** on Barrett Drive, on the southeast side of town, is named after Harold Lasseter, a local legend who perished in the desert searching for a fabled reef of gold in 1931. Harry should have lived so long; the gold is here, on the gaming tables. The casino also has a disco open Thursday 11:00 p.m. to 4:00 a.m., Friday and Saturday 11:00 p.m. to 5:00 a.m.

There's live music Thursday to Sunday at the **Todd Tavern,** Wills Terrace and Todd Street Mall, and the **Stuart Arms Hotel,** Parsons Street and Todd Street Mall. **Bojangles Nightclub**, Todd Street near Stott Terrace is open nightly except Sunday for meals and disco dancing 'til the wee hours.

If there's more highbrow entertainment in town, you'll find it at the **Araluen Arts Centre,** west of the centre on Larapinta Drive. The Alice's centre for the performing and visual arts attracts big name entertainers from Australia and overseas.

TOUR 12

ALICE SPRINGS TO AYERS ROCK

Marvel at the weird geology of the Red Centre as you fly from
Alice Springs to Yulara resort village at Ayers Rock, arriving in
the early afternoon. After getting settled in your lodging and
exploring the community, join the sunset barbecue tour to The
Olgas.

Suggested schedule

9:00	You'll have time to do some shopping or sightseeing in Alice Springs before taking a shuttle bus to the airport.
11:35	Ansett N.T. Flight BT278 for Ayers Rock.
12:20	Arrive at Ayers Rock's Connellan Airport.
1:00	Get settled in your accommodation, take a dip in the pool, then drop by the Yulara Visitors' Centre and tour the resort complex.
4:30	Depart on 'Outback' barbecue-tour to the Olgas.
9:30	Return to hotel.

Ayers Rock orientation

The great red monolith of Ayers Rock is the symbol of the
Australian Outback, at once an irresistable spiritual force to the
Aboriginal people and a testimony to the stark primeval beauty of
the desert landscape.

There is no larger rock on earth. Yet Ayers Rock may not be as
well known for its massive size (1,260 feet high, 5½ miles around
its base) as for its moods. From dawn to dusk, the Rock
undergoes a continuous series of subtle colour changes, from
sunrise pink to midday brown, sunset red to post-sunset purple.
During the rare desert downpours, it can even appear silvery with
rain cascading down its time-sculptured slopes.

The ancient Loritja and Pitjantjatjara tribes called the Rock
'Uluru'. Thousands of years ago, they decorated the cave walls
around its base with paintings and petroglyphs. Not until 1872
did Europeans know of the Rock; Ernest Giles sighted it during
his explorations of the Centre, and the following year, William
Gosse led a three-month camel caravan to climb the monolith.
Today, the ascent is a relatively simple, if strenuous, morning
excursion.

About 510 square miles surrounding Ayers Rock and the nearby Olgas range, piled high like a giant's marbles above the sandy earth, were established in 1958 as Ayers Rock-Mount Olga National Park. Title for the parklands was transferred to the Aboriginal people in 1985, and Uluru National Park came into being. Commercial enterprise — motels, a campground and an airstrip — was moved out of the shadow of the Rock at that time. A new resort village, Yulara, was created outside the northern boundary of the park, 19 km (12 miles) from the Rock.

Yulara was built to provide comfort in the desert sun for the rapidly growing influx of tourists. Only 2,300 people visited Ayers Rock when the national park first opened in 1958; but by 1987, with a tarmacked, 468 km (291 miles) all-weather road linking the Rock to Alice Springs, Uluru was attracting 220,000 visitors from all over the world — despite being one of the costliest destinations in Australia.

The resort village can accommodate up to 5,000 people a day in two luxury hotels, a mid-priced lodge and a spacious campground. And it is a complete village — in fact, with its resident population of around 500, it is the third largest community in the sparsely settled Northern Territory (after Darwin and Alice Springs). There's a small shopping square, a school, a medical centre, a community hall and sports centre, a police station, and other facilities to keep the people from feeling too isolated.

Still, they must cope with the summer heat and year-round temperature extremes. From December to February, daytime temperatures average about 97 degrees Fahrenheit, dropping to around 70 at night; mid-winter temperatures range from average daytime highs of 58 to nightime lows of 41, though freezing temperatures are not uncommon. Total rainfall is only 10 inches a year, with February the wettest month (1½ inches) and September the driest (¼ inch).

Yulara transport

There isn't any cheap way to get around here, short of walking. The shuttle bus for the short hop from the airport to Yulara costs A$5 (£2.40) one way; the price of the three-times-a-day shuttle from the resort to Ayers Rock is A$12 (£5.70) return, or about 50 cents (23p) a mile. And so it goes. The Ayers Rock Touring Co. has the concession. Some visitors find the three-day 'Rock Pass', allowing unlimited trips on the shuttle buses to the Rock and the Olgas, a worthwhile purchase at A$39 (£18.50).

Cars are available for hire, but they're hardly a bargain. If the weather cooperates — and it usually does — consider hiring a moped from the Mobil Service Station in Yulara village. Half-day (four-hour) rental is A$20 (£9.50), full-day A$30 (£14.25).

Where to stay

The **Sheraton Ayers Rock Hotel** (tel. 56-2200) is the luxury
leader, with 230 rooms rambling around a lovely swimming pool
and courtyard. Twin rooms are A$135 (£64) a night. Many
visitors prefer the A$120 (£57) rooms across the village at the
Four Seasons Ayers Rock Motel (tel. 56-2100). From these
two inns, it's an abrupt step down-market to the **Ayers Rock
Lodge** (tel. 56-2170), offering bare-bones family units or cabins for
four at $A48 (£23), hostel-style dormitory accommodation at A$12
(£5.70) a bunk.

Where to eat

The **Sheraton** has two fine restaurants, the **Four Seasons**
another. At either hotel, you can get a filling buffet dinner for
around A$25 (£12). There are three less expensive options,
perhaps the best being the counter meals and buffet at the
Ernest Giles Tavern, open daily in the Shopping Square. The
adjacent **Old Oak Tree Coffee Shop** has light meals and
takeaways, while the **Ayers Rock Lodge Food Bar** is popular
for its casual home cooking.

Sightseeing highlight

● ● **The Olgas,** to many visitors, are even more spectacular
than Ayers Rock itself. An accumulation of 36 oddly shaped
domes that rise from the Central Australian desert some 32 km
(20 miles) west of the Rock, they were known to the Aboriginals
as Katatjuta and feared as hungry giants. Indeed, the Olgas can
be sirens who lure explorers into their seductive wonderland only
to cook them alive in a midday oven.

By late afternoon, the heat is off again. One way to appreciate
these geological curiosities is with the Ayers Rock Touring
Company's 'Evening in the Outback' tour. You'll be picked up in
Yulara about 4:30 p.m., head out to the west side of the Olgas to
watch the colourful sunset, then drive to an isolated spot for a
'steak-and-snags' barbecue under the Southern Cross. If you shine
a flashlight toward the darkness around your campfire, you may
see the shining eyes of wild dingoes waiting to feast on your
leftovers. The tour's major drawback is its price – A$39 (£18.50),
not acceptable on the Rock Pass. (Hours are a half-hour later
from mid-October to March.)

Nightlife

A bush band performs Aussie sing-along and dance music most
nights in the Sheraton's **Mulgara Bar.** It's good fun, the best
reason to visit the Sheraton if you're not staying there. The
Ernest Giles Tavern has a pub disco several nights of the week.

TOUR 13
AYERS ROCK

Learn about the Aboriginal culture today. Spend the morning
with a native guide who will show you how his people found
food, water, shelter and medicine in this arid landscape. Visit the
craft exhibit at the Uluru National Park ranger station and search
for ancient petroglyphs in caves around the base of Ayers Rock.
Back at Yulara, sip champagne as you watch the sun set over the
red rock.

Suggested schedule

7:00	Leave Yulara via shuttle bus for Ayers Rock.
7.30	While others are beginning their ascent, stroll to Maggie Springs, then to the ranger station.
8:30	'Liru' walk with Aboriginal guide.
10:45	Return to the ranger station to see the outdoor exhibit of Aboriginal crafts and video.
12:15	Back to Yulara aboard shuttle bus.
1:00	Lunch, swim, relax.
Open	Go to the Sheraton lookout tower 45 minutes before sunset to sip champagne and watch the Rock's colours change. Then dinner.
9:00	Early bedtime for tomorrow's 'ordeal'.

Sightseeing highlights
● ● **Maggie Springs,** known to the Pitjantjatjara as Mutitjulu,
is a deep, tranquil pool nestled against the southeast wall of Ayers
Rock. After a rainstorm, you can often see tiny desert frogs and
fairy shrimp in the water. The hideaway is especially striking in
the late morning, when the blue of the Outback sky contrasts
sharply with the red of the rock and the green of the mulga and
desert oak vegetation. Nearby are several small caves, their walls
and roofs adorned with Aboriginal cave paintings thousands of
years old. Maggie Springs are a level 2½ km walk from the
shuttle bus stop.
● ● **The Liru Walk** only happens twice a week, but it's worth
catching when it does. Beginning at 8:30 a.m. Tuesdays and
Thursdays, an Aboriginal woman (females are the traditional food-
gatherers in Central Australia) leads a group from the Uluru

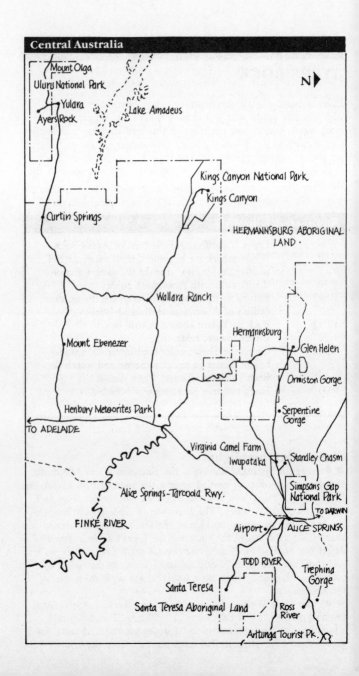

Central Australia

Mount Olga
Uluru National Park
Yulara
Ayers Rock
Lake Amadeus

N▶

Kings Canyon National Park
Kings Canyon

Curtin Springs

· HERMANNSBURG ABORIGINAL LAND ·

Wallara Ranch

Hermannsburg
Glen Helen

Mount Ebenezer

Ormiston Gorge

Henbury Meteorites Park

Serpentine Gorge

TO ADELAIDE

Virginia Camel Farm
Iwupataka

Standley Chasm

Alice Springs–Tarcoola Rwy.

Simpsons Gap National Park

TO DARWIN

FINKE RIVER

Airport

ALICE SPRINGS

TODD RIVER

Trephina Gorge

Santa Teresa
Santa Teresa Aboriginal Land

Ross River

Arltunga Tourist Pk.

National Park Ranger Station on a two-hour bush walk to
demonstrate how her people survived in this arid climate using
only natural food sources. You'll learn, for instance, that the
burrowing witchety grub is superb food, 50% protein and 50%
fat; that the fruit of the plumbush tree has the highest known
concentration of Vitamin C; that the prolific mulga tree has seeds
that can be ground to make flour; and that the flowers of the
hakea tree, mixed with water, make a drink similar to cola. And
remember that scene in 'Crocodile Dundee' where Mick skewers a
large lizard for dinner? Your guide will show you where to find a
tasty sand goanna just like it.

In fact, there is a bewildering variety of wildlife here in the
desert. Naturalists have counted 290 species of plant life, 151
birds, 52 reptiles and 22 native mammals. The most prolific of all
creatures is the blowfly, a sort of larger, more persistent version
of the housefly. Without direct sunlight, and with a bit of a
breeze, they're not bad. In most circumstances they're extemely
unpleasant. You'll soon learn why 'The Great Australian Salute'
is a hand waving past your face to keep these flies out of your
eyes, nose, ears and mouth.

Flies notwithstanding, the Liru Walk is a fascinating look at a
lifestyle very different from our own. Tour numbers are limited,
so book ahead by phoning 56-2988. The tour concludes at the
base of the Rock climb, leaving a 20-minute return walk to the
ranger station.

● **Uluru National Park Ranger Station,** where everyone who
enters the park is supposed to stop and pay a A$1.50 (70p) use
fee, has a number of exhibits of special interest to the park
visitor. In particular, take some time to talk with the Aboriginal
people displaying local, hand-made arts and crafts in a special
outdoor area.

TOUR 14

AYERS ROCK TO WALLARA RANCH

If the world's largest monolith is awesome at sunset, it's even more stunning at dawn. Wake early to watch the spectacle, and to beat the heat and flies as you scale the huge Red Rock. Then you too can wear a T-shirt declaring: 'I Climbed Ayers Rock'. After lunch, board a bus for the 125-mile drive to Wallara Ranch, where you'll spend the night at an Outback station.

Suggested schedule

6:45	Leave Yulara via shuttle bus for Ayers Rock.
7:30	Begin climb up Ayers Rock. Allow 90 minutes for the return trip.
9:00	Tour base of Rock by bus, or preferably, with ranger guide to Kantju Gorge.
11:45	Return to Yulara via shuttle bus. Lunch.
1:30	Farewell to Ayers Rock.
3:30	Rest stop at Angas Downs turnoff.
5:30	Arrive Wallara Ranch for overnight stay.

Sightseeing highlights

● ● ● **Climbing Ayers Rock** is a must, as long as you're in reasonably good physical condition. The ever-cautious national park administration warns that the average time of climbing the 1.6 km (1 mile) to the cairn and returning to the foot of the Rock is two hours. As a slightly out-of-shape, over-the-hill hiker, I can accomplish it in a little over an hour, including 15 minutes or so relaxing and taking photos at the top. But don't push yourself too hard; if you feel exhausted or nauseous, quit. Take a break, then head back down.

The first 500 metres of the climb are the steepest. A staunch chain has been sunk into the Rock to provide a handhold for any and all who need it while ascending the 45 to 60-degree angle. Once that portion has been surmounted, it's merely an uphill walk, with just a couple of precipitous drops and rises across eroded ridges.

At the top, you'll be rewarded with an unfettered view of hundreds of miles of red dirt. Be sure to sign the climbers' register, noting the vast array of nationalities who have put their home address there next to your own. After a short rest, you can head back down. Your calves got a workout on the way up; now your thighs will feel it. Some climbers find it easier to back down the chain on the steepest stretch.

The best shoes for climbing are rubber-soled. Any kind of training shoes work as well as proper climbing boots. Don't go in street shoes, sandals or bare feet. Bring something with you to drink, and if you're starting much later than 8:00 a.m., put on suntan lotion and a sun hat. The wind can be stiff on the rock, so be sure to tie down anything you carry—or it may wind up at the bottom of the Rock long before you do.

● **Circling the Rock** aboard the shuttle bus can be done if you're back at the base by 9:00 a.m. The driver-guide points out Taputji (Little Ayers Rock), Maggie Springs and other sites around the Rock's circumference en route back to Yulara. It's interesting to note how different Ayers Rock appears from different aspects. The tour costs A$15 (£7.15) including the A$12 (£5.70) shuttle fee from Yulara.

● **Ranger-guided walks,** which also leave at 9:00 a.m. from the car park at the base of the Rock climb, are free. For over an hour, hikers accompany a park ranger into Kantju Gorge, a cleft in the Rock with an adjacent waterhole. The ranger explains Ayers Rock's place in Aboriginal legend, and tells about the geology and environment of this Central Australian region.

● ● **Ayers Rock-Kings Canyon tours** are conducted by several tour companies based in Alice Springs. Any Northern Territory Government Tourist Bureau can provide a complete listing. I like the low-budget tour offered by A-1/Spinifex Tours (write Fan Arcade, Todd Street Mall, Alice Springs, NT 5750, tel. 089/52-5424 or 52-2203). But its tours are Saturday-to-Monday and Tuesday-to-Thursday expeditions, not helpful to those of us leaving Yulara on a Friday. My second choice is Ansett Trailways (Todd and Parsons Streets, Alice Springs, NT 5750, tel. 089/52-2422), which has daily departures on the three-day Alice–Ayers Rock–Kings Canyon–Alice circuit. The trick is to join a tour in progress on departure from Yulara. Advance arrangements are essential.

You'll leave Yulara on the Lasseter Highway, a 247 km (153 mile) thoroughfare connecting Ayers Rock with the Stuart Highway, the main north–south route from Adelaide to Darwin. About 138 km (86 miles) from Yulara, following a rest stop at the Curtin Springs homestead and a view of isolated Mount Connor, you'll turn north past Angas Downs to the Wallara Ranch, 70 km (43 miles) further.

Wallara Ranch offers bunkhouse and private, four-to-a-room cabin accommodation for economy prices. There's also a dining room with filling, country-style meals.

TOUR 15

WALLARA RANCH TO ALICE SPRINGS

Scramble through the sheer walls of colourful Kings Canyon, then return to Alice Springs in the evening. If you're not totally exhausted, enjoy a nightcap at the casino.

Suggested schedule

6:00	Rise and shine; eat breakfast.
7:00	Leave for Kings Canyon.
9:00	Explore the spectacular chasm. Wander through the lush Garden of Eden and climb to the canyon rim for marvellous panoramic views.
11:30	Leave Kings Canyon.
1:30	Lunch at Wallara Ranch.
3:00	Leave for Alice Springs.
5:00	See the Henbury Craters.
6:30	Arrive at Alice Springs for the night.

Sightseeing highlights

● ● ● **Kings Canyon**—Australia's spectacular 'Grand Canyon' is a deep cleft in the George Gill Ranges, about 250 km—155 air miles—southwest of Alice Springs. (From the Wallara Ranch it's a 99-km, or 61-mile, drive each way.)

Sheer sandstone walls rising 700 to 900 feet above the canyon floor vary in hue from pink to crimson, ivory to deep purple. In the Garden of Eden, lush palms grow around dozens of waterholes, reflecting the multi-coloured walls like so many kaleidoscopes. In the Lost City, rocky outcrops look like primitive rock dwellings of a forgotten tribe. The Sphinx is another formation unique in this terrain. You may find rock wallabies and goanna lizards at the waterholes, and you'll certainly see rose-tinted galahs and a variety of other birds.

It's a steep climb to the canyon rim—more difficult than the struggle up Ayers Rock—but the panoramic views from the summit make the climb worthwhile. As at the Rock, you should wear rubber-soled shoes for climbing, apply suntan lotion, wear a sun hat, and carry something to drink.

Kings Canyon Road runs the 198 km (123 miles) from the canyon to the Stuart Highway, via the midway stop at Wallara Ranch. This is a graded-dirt road, typical of the Outback. Tour

bus drivers who ply this route regularly have taken all appropriate
precautions for Outback travel, but if you're driving yourself you
should follow the old Boy Scout axiom and 'Be Prepared'.

Watch out for road flooding, particularly where it crosses the
Palmer River. This arid land doesn't absorb rainfall quickly, so
even a half-inch of precipitation can have a major effect on road
conditions. Beware of collisions with kangaroos, wild camels and
brumbies (wild horses). Carry water—at least a gallon per person
per day of your trip—plus reserve petrol, a tool kit, two spare
tyres and extra engine parts. It helps if you have a mechanical
inclination.

● **Henbury Craters** are an odd cluster of about a dozen meteor
craters off Kings Canyon Road near its junction with the Stuart
Highway, 132 km (82 miles) south of Alice Springs. Between
2,000 and 3,000 years ago, a shower of meteorites rained down
upon this 40-acre conservation park, creating craters from 20 to
600 feet across and as much as 50 feet deep. A walking trail from
the car park signposts many of the features.

● **The Virginia Camel Farm**, 90 km (56 miles) south of the
Alice, is Noel Fullerton's contribution to Central Australian
culture. Fullerton originated Alice Springs' Lions Club 'Camel
Cup' in the 1970s, won it himself four times, and now has placed
his teenage children in the championship category of camel-riding.
(The Cup races are held annually in May.) The farm domesticates
some of the Centre's estimated 15,000 wild camels and breeds
others for export to—of all places—the Arab world, from which
Australia's herd originated! Visitors can pay a few dollars for a
short camel ride, or book a one or two-week safari east into the
Rainbow Valley.

TOUR 16

ALICE SPRINGS TO CAIRNS

Today, fly from Alice Springs to Cairns. On arrival in Cairns, the
humidity will tell you immediately that you're in the tropics.
Have a cold beer at an Esplanade pub, watch the fishing and
pleasure boats return from the Great Barrier Reef, see the Reef
World aquarium. For dinner, order barramundi, a delectable
river-run cod.

Suggested schedule

8:30	Leisurely breakfast at hotel, then take a shuttle bus to the airport.
10:55	Ansett Flight 285 to Cairns.
1:20	Arrive at Cairns International Airport. Take a shuttle bus 8 km to town and check into hotel.
3:00	Stroll down the Esplanade and around town. See the Reef World aquarium, the marlin jetty, and perhaps the museum or House of 10,000 Shells.
6:30	Dinner at one of Cairn's fine seafood eateries.

Cairns orientation

Cairns (don't pronounce the 'r') is the undeclared capital of lazy,
tropical North Queensland. A rapidly growing town of about
70,000 people on the shores of Trinity Bay, it is wedged against a
backdrop of rainforest-clad mountains, facing the so-called eighth
wonder of the world, the Great Barrier Reef.

Founded in the mid-1870s as a customs collection point and a
port for gold and tin mines in the interior of Queensland, it later
grew as a centre for sugar-cane growing and processing. Sugar
and tin remain economically important today, along with fishing,
timber and tropical fruit.

But tourism is taking over as the No. 1 revenue producer. Why
do the tourists come? The primary reason is the Reef. No
population centre along the Australian coast is closer to the coral
phenomenon than Cairns, with Green Island a mere 40-minute
launch trip away. Second, they come for the fishing. Cairns is
famed for its sportfishing fleet. Third, they come for the jungle,
some of the last great tracts of rain forest on earth are west of
Cairns, on the Atherton Tableland, and north, around Cape
Tribulation.

Cairns itself is an easy town to find your way around. It's stereotypically tropical, its ornate wide-verandahed homes often raised well above the ground for air circulation. The streets are wide and palm-fringed, the harbour a bustling centre of trade amid squawking sea birds. Spence Street runs due west from the marlin jetty; it's paralleled to the north by Shields, Aplin, Florence, Minnie and Upward Streets. The Esplanade, which runs along the shore from Upward Street to Spence Street, and McLeod Street, which fronts the railway tracks, mark the eastern and western boundaries of the central district. Abbott, Lake, Grafton and Sheridan Streets run between, from east to west. City Place, a shopping arcade marking the centre of the city, is at the intersection of Shields Street and Lake Street. Sheridan Street is the main thoroughfare north toward the airport and the Cook Highway.

City transport

A regular shuttle-bus service operates between Cairns International Airport and town, a distance of 8 km (5 miles), for A$3 (£1.40). (Leaving town, call 53-4722 for pickup times.) Taxi fare between Cairns and the airport is about A$7 (£3.33).

If you arrived in Cairns by train from Brisbane or other points south, you'll disembark at Cairns Station on McLeod Street, at the end of Shields Street. All central points are within easy walking distance. (The economy single adult rail fare from Brisbane to Cairns, one-way, is A$84.80 (£40). Trains arrive

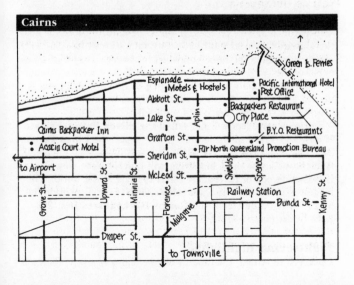

Tuesday to Friday plus Sunday at 7:45 p.m.; the Queenslander express comes in Monday only at 5:55 p.m.)

A variety of bus services are available within and around Cairns at reasonable fares. (Schedules are posted in the foyer of the O.T. Corporation and on the window of Rockman's, both on Shields Street between City Place and Abbott Street.) There are interstate bus stations for Greyhound at 78 Grafton Street and Ansett Pioneer at 58 Shields Street.

Hire cars are also readily available in town and at the airport. For cheap moke or moped rentals, check with Mini Car Rental, 143 Sheridan Street. You can hire bicycles in several locations, including Cycle Works, Aplin and Lake Streets, and the Bicycle Barn, 61 Sheridan Street.

Where to stay

There's a wide variety of accommodation available in Cairns. Generally speaking, you'll find the budget and moderate lodging in the town itself. Luxury hotels are often up the coast, the best currently being the **Ramada Reef Resort** at Palm Cove (tel. 070/55-3999), about 25 km (16 miles) north of Cairns. It is dwarfed by Sheraton's A\$150 million (£71 million) **Four Mile Beach Resort**, 76 km (47 miles) from Cairns at Port Douglas, opened in late 1987 with an 18-hole championship golf course and hovercraft connection to Cairns International Airport.

The No. 1 hotel in Cairns is the **Pacific International Hotel**, 43 The Esplanade (tel. 070/51-7888), with three restaurants, three bars and a health club. Its pre-eminence is challenged by a new **Hilton** and a new **Park Royal**.

In the moderate price class, it would be hard to do better than the **Cairns Colonial Club**, 18–26 Cannon Street (tel. 53-5111), which surmounts the minor drawback of being a couple of miles north of the city centre with regular free shuttle service. A choice of rooms at several price levels starting at A\$49 (£23.30) are nestled around an open-air restaurant-bar and saltwater pool, complete with sandy beach and waterfall.

Economy travellers will do well at the **Silver Palms Private Hotel**, 153 The Esplanade (tel. 51-2059), and the **Linga Longa**, 223 The Esplanade (tel. 51-3013), both equipped with kitchens. And those touring on a shoestring will quickly learn why Cairns is becoming one of the budget travel capitals of the world. The biggest of five hostels is **Caravella's**, 77-81 The Esplanade (tel. 51-2159). A bit quieter is the **Cairns Backpackers Inn**, 255 Lake Street (tel. 51-9166).

Sightseeing highlights

Once you're settled, it's time to see the sights of town. Cairns is

better known as a base for excursions to the Reef and inland, but
these will fill an afternoon.

● ● **The Marlin Jetty** is a 'must' stop during the sportfishing
season, which runs from August into December. When private
boats and charter operators return here toward evening with their
days' catches, the heart of even the veteran fisherman has to
thump a little. Black marlin, hoisted onto the scales, may go well
over the 1,000 pound mark.

● **Reef World** is an aquarium on Martin Parade with a variety
of saltwater species—crocodiles, turtles, sharks, giant clams, and a
great many fish, including barramundi, huge groupers and the
poisonous stonefish. There's even a stingray which is fed by hand
every day at 2:00 p.m. Open daily from 10:00 a.m. to 5:30 p.m.;
admission is A$3 (£1.40).

● **Windows on the Reef**, located off Wharf Street on the Great
Barrier Reef cruise docks, simulates a night dive on the reef from
within a small rotating theatre. The 45-minute show is a good
introduction to the massive coral creation not far off shore. Open
daily 10:00 a.m. to 5:30 p.m. Admission is A$4 (£1.90).

● **The Cairns Museum**, located in an early 20th century
School of Arts building at the corner of Lake and Shields Streets,
has displays of natural history, North Queensland Aboriginal
artifacts, gold-mining (and early Chinese habitation) and railway
construction. Open 10:00 a.m. to 3:00 p.m. Monday to Friday.
Admission is A$1 (45p).

Cairns Botanical Gardens, Collins Avenue in Edge Hill, two
miles from the town centre, comprise a luxuriant century-old
tropical jungle and parkland with more than 10,000 species of
trees, shrubs and flowers. There's a great view across Cairns to
Trinity Bay from the top of Mount Whitfield. Open daily sunrise
to sunset. Admission is free.

Where to eat

For a relatively small city, Cairns offers an awesome variety of
international cuisine in its many restaurants.

Some of the licensed seafood restaurants have the most style.
Try **Scuppers**, Grafton and Aplin Streets; **Fathoms**, Grove and
Diggers Streets (near Grafton), especially for the garlic chili crab;
or **Tawny's** on the Marlin Jetty. **Lin Nam**, 14 Aplin Street, has
good Chinese seafood. An excellent BYO seafood eatery is
Avocado, 228 Sheridan Street.

Among other BYO restaurants, these are a few of the best, by
cuisine: **Der Feinschmecker** (German), 95 Grafton Street;
Thuggee Bill's (Indian), 42 Aplin Street; **Toko Baru**
(Indonesian), 42 Spence Street; **Omar Khayyam** (Lebanese), 82
Sheridan Street, **Rahmah's** (Malaysian), 47 Shields Street; **Little**

Gringo (Mexican), 95 Grafton Street; **Casa Gomez** (Spanish), 48
Aplin Street; **Sweethearts** (vegetarian), Rusty's Bazaar on
Grafton Street. Along the Esplanade and around the City Place
arcade, several restaurants have outdoor tables set up to catch the
eyes and noses of passers-by. One of the most popular for lunch
is **Swagman's Rest,** City Place.

Last, but far from least, is the **Backpackers' Restaurant** on
Shields Street just east of City Place. With a name like that, its
clientele is—you guessed it—mainly backpackers. And it's always
packed. Counter meals are cheap and good, beer is cheap and
good, and both are served into the wee hours.

Nightlife

The scene changes often in a resort town like Cairns, but at the
time of writing, the favoured upmarket nightclubs were the
Playpen International, 2 Lake Street; **Scandals**, in the
Tradewinds Sunlodge at Lake and Florence Streets; and the
House on the Hill, Kingsford Street in out-of-the-way
Mooroobool. All are open until 3 in the morning, although nights
of closing vary.

Close to the city centre, and more in the vein of a quieter drink
and conversation to a piano bar or light jazz, are **The Nest**, 82
McLeod Street; **Duke's**, upstairs at 86 Lake Street; and
Kipling's Wine Bar, 79 Abbott Street.

Young rockers find loud music and cheap drinks at the
Hideaway Tavern, Lake Street between Spence and Shields
Streets. **Hides Hotel**, at the southwest corner of City Place, is
always good for a party. You'll often find the fishermen in the
Marlin Bar at the Great Northern Hotel, 69 Abbott Street.

You might also get a kick out of **Milliway's**, an upstairs BYO
built around the theme of Douglas Adams's space novel, *A
Hitchhikers' Guide to the Galaxy.* This BYO cafe upstairs at 144
Grafton Street offers a place where any travelling musician can
drop by to jam for all he (or she) is worth.

Helpful hints

The two best sources of travel and touring information once
you've arrived in Cairns are the Far North Queensland Promotion
Bureau, corner of Sheridan and Aplin Streets (tel. 51-3588), and
the Queensland Government Travel Centre, 12 Shields Street (tel.
51-4066). Both are open weekdays 9:00 a.m. to 5:00 p.m.

The General Post Office is on the corner of Florence and
Sheridan Streets. Banks stay open from 9:30 a.m. to 4:00 p.m.
Monday to Thursday, to 5:00 p.m. Friday. Shops in the central
area open 8:30 a.m. to 5:15 p.m. Monday to Thursday, to 9:00
p.m. Friday, to noon Saturday.

TOUR 17

GREEN ISLAND

Ship out for Green Island, a tiny coral cay 40 minutes' cruise
offshore where you can swim, study sea life from a glass-bottom
boat, view the world's largest crocodile in captivity, and dine,
drink and sleep at the small resort.

Suggested schedule

7:00	Breakfast at hotel. Stow whatever bags you won't need on the island to await your return tomorrow night.
8:30	Leave for Green Island aboard Hayles' Cruises 220-passenger catamaran.
11:00	Walk around the island. It takes 20 minutes.
12:00	Lie on the beach.
1:00	Lunch, if you're ready.
2:30	Siesta.
3:30	Snorkelling again, or visit the croc.
6:00	Happy hour.
7:00	Dinner.

Alternative schedule for budget travellers

9:00	Leave for Fitzroy Island aboard the *MV Fitzroy* catamaran.
9:45	Arrive at Fitzroy Island. Snorkel over the coral or go bushwalking in the rainforest.
1:00	Lunch. Rest of day on the beach at Fitzroy.

Sightseeing highlights

● ● ● **Green Island** is a misnomer. It's green, all right, cloaked
in lush palms, figs and other rainforest vegetation, but at a mere
32 acres in size, and nowhere more than 10 feet in elevation, it's
hardly classifiable as an island! In fact, you can walk around this
isolated coral cay, 17 miles offshore from Cairns, in about 20
minutes. But Green Island's miniature size is part of its charm.
Most of the islet is reserved as a marine national park for its fine
plant and bird life. It's completely fringed by a beach of fine
white sand, and the offshore snorkelling is excellent.

   Hayles' Cruises (tel. 51-5644) operate a transit service from
the Green Island Jetty off Wharf Street opposite Abbott Street.
Luxury catamarans—double-deckers complete with bars—leave at

8:30 and 10:30 a.m. daily on the 40-minute journey. The adult
fare is A$23 (£11) return. Ordinary launches leave at 9:00 a.m.
daily, making the trip in 90 minutes for A$12 (£5.70) return.

Once on the island, what's there to do? Well, to begin with,
there's that fabulous beach. Swim, snorkel, skin dive, even try
windsurfing. (Equipment is available for hire at reasonable rates
on the beach.) You can try casting a line for reef fish, or just
commune with nature in the forest.

At the end of the boat jetty, anchored on the seabed, is the
Green Island Underwater Observatory, where you can
descend to the ocean floor to gaze through large viewing windows
at luminescent tropical fish flitting through colourful banks of
coral, itself inhabited by starfish, anemones, giant clams and other
undersea creatures. Admission is A$3.20 (£1.50).

On shore, **Marineland Melanesia** is an indoor-outdoor
aquarium combined with a New Guinean artifact collection. It's
worth visiting mainly to see its crocodiles. Well over a dozen of
the ill-tempered reptiles are in residence here, including one
Guinness-class monster nearly 20 feet long. He usually hides
under his lily pads, but one glimpse of his huge jaws thrashing
after a chunk of raw meat at feeding time will remind you why
you should never go swimming alone in a saltwater estuary.
Admission is A$3.50 (£1.70). Next door to this Marineland is the
Castaway Theatre, which offers an underwater camera's
perspective of the wonders of the Great Barrier Reef.

The comfortable **Green Island Reef Resort** has private
lodging for A$54 to A$69 (£25 to £33) a night ($10 (£4.75) more
in the mid-summer holiday season). The price includes dinner
(usually a choice of meat or a reef fish) and a buffet breakfast.
Lunch at the outdoor grill and drinks in the lounge are extra.

●● **Fitzroy Island**—Fitzroy is a much larger island than
Green—about 750 acres—but a much smaller resort. That makes
it ideal for travellers seeking a bit of isolation.

Located 3½ miles off the coast 16 miles east of Cairns, this
mountainous island is shrouded in tropical rainforest and fringed
by rugged coral beaches. It's not great for sunbathing, but there's
an excellent reef 150 feet offshore for snorkelling and diving. You
can hire equipment for those sports as well as canoeing and
paddle skiing. Or you can go off on your own long bushwalks
through the dense vegetation.

The *MV Fitzroy* catamaran (A$11 (£5.25) return) leaves Cairns
daily at 9:00 a.m., reaching Fitzroy at 9:45 a.m. It departs Fitzroy
at 1:30 p.m. for passage back to Cairns via Green Island.

The **Fitzroy Island Resort** on Welcome Bay caters to budget
travellers with hostel-style rooms (A$25 (£12) for two) with
communal kitchens. It also has guest villas for $79 (£38) full
board ($90 (£43) single).

TOUR 18

GREAT BARRIER REEF

You'll leave Green Island this morning to spend the day snorkell-ing or diving on the outer Barrier Reef. It is an incredible experience to see more than 200 species of tropical reef fish swimming through an undersea 'garden' of multicoloured coral. Return to Cairns at night.

Suggested schedule

11:15	Leave Green Island aboard Hayles' *Reef Cat* for Michaelmas Cay and Hastings Reef.
12:15	Arrive at Hastings Reef.
3:15	Leave Hastings Reef.
5:15	Return to Cairns after 15-minute pick-up and drop-off stop at Green Island.
5:30	Get re-established at hotel.
6:30	Dinner, perhaps followed by tropical nightlife.

Alternative schedule (for Fitzroy Island overnighters)

1:30	Depart Fitzroy Island.
2:00	Arrive Green Island.
4:30	Leave Green Island.
5:15	Return to Cairns. Remainder of day as above.

Sightseeing highlights

● ● ● **The Great Barrier Reef** is truly one of the wonders of the world. Stretching for more than 2,000 km (1,250 miles) down the coast of Queensland from New Guinea to the Tropic of Capricorn, it is the largest structure (80,000 square miles of individual reefs, shoals and islets) ever created by living creatures.

Tiny marine animals called polyps (closely related to sea anemones) are the master engineers. Forming colonies linked by a network of tubes and protected by an external skeleton of lime, they forever grow upon the mass remains of their forebears. Their formations are as varied in colour as in shape, from red fans to yellow staghorn, purple 'brains' to green cabbage, and many, many more.

Snorkelling or diving in the Reef is like taking a swim through an underwater garden. I've put on a mask and fins in bodies of water all over the world, from Hawaii to the Indian Ocean, but never have I been more astounded than on the Barrier Reef.

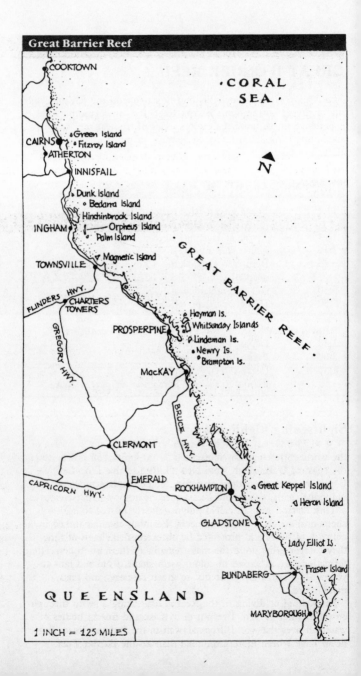

Great Barrier Reef

COOKTOWN

•CORAL
SEA•

• Green Island
• Fitzroy Island
CAIRNS
ATHERTON
INNISFAIL

• Dunk Island
• Bedarra Island
Hinchinbrook Island
INGHAM — Orpheus Island
Palm Island
Magnetic Island
TOWNSVILLE

N

GREAT BARRIER REEF

FLINDERS HWY.
CHARTERS
TOWERS

GREGORY HWY.

Hayman Is.
Whitsunday Islands
PROSPERPINE
Lindeman Is.
Newry Is.
Brampton Is.

MacKAY

BRUCE HWY.

CLERMONT

CAPRICORN HWY.
EMERALD
ROCKHAMPTON
Great Keppel Island

Heron Island

GLADSTONE

Lady Elliot Is.

BUNDABERG
Fraser Island

QUEENSLAND

MARYBOROUGH

1 INCH = 125 MILES

More than 1,400 species of fish have been identified here, each seemingly brighter and more fanciful than the next. There are turtles and rays, starfish and sea urchins, jellyfish and giant clams, and more.

The polyps' only known enemy, by the way—besides the polluting or vandalising human—is the crown-of-thorns starfish. This creature is a formidable foe indeed, one posing a real challenge to marine biologists trying to control the escalating degeneration of parts of the Reef.

The best place from which to approach the underwater wonderland of the Great Barrier Reef is right where you are now. At its southern end, the Reef is nearly 160 km (100 miles) from the Queensland coast near Rockhampton, and it takes a long boat trip (or a seaplane hop) to reach it. From Cairns, it's but a 20 to 30-km (12 to 20-mile) trip from the Australian mainland to the inner edge of the Reef.

●● **Michaelmas Cay**, 45 km (28 miles) northeast of Cairns, is of particular note among the reef islets because it is a tern rookery. Thousands of the squawking sea birds circle overhead, protecting their young in their nests, and squabble over shellfish on the isle's sands. (Visitors may carry umbrellas to protect themselves from smelly aerial assaults.) The cay also has superb diving on the offshore Reef.

A Hayles' Cruises launch leaves the Green Island Jetty daily at 8:30 a.m., stops at Green Island for two hours, then continues to Michaelmas Cay. A buffet lunch, snorkelling gear and rides on a submarine-like-reef viewer are provided free to all who pay the A$54 fare (£25).

●●● **Hastings Reef** lies on the Reef's outer fringe, where the coral is the youngest and the variety and colour of marine life is the greatest. Don't let cloudy weather put you off a trip to this submarine phenomenon, 55 km (34 miles) northeast of Cairns. For one thing, you might not burn as quickly in the less-than-sunny skies. For another, the filtration of rays through the clouds actually brings out the Reef's colours better, especially the blues.

Hayles' Outer Barrier Reef cruise leaves Cairns at 8:30 a.m. daily, stops for two hours at Green Island (where it is joined by Green Island overnighters), does a slow circle around Michaelmas Cay, then anchors at Hastings Reef for three hours. An all-inclusive fare of A$65 (£81) includes a buffet lunch, morning and afternoon tea, snorkelling gear (and instruction from a professional dive team), rides on the *Reef Pioneer* subsea coral viewer and video films of Reef life. Scuba diving equipment can be rented by qualified divers.

TOUR 19

CAIRNS TO BRISBANE

The scenic Kuranda Railway will take you inland to the edge of
the rainforested Atherton Tableland, climbing steeply above fields
of sugar cane to the Barron River Gorge. In Kuranda, you'll have
time to see Barron Falls, the open-air market and the Noctarium
before returning to Cairns after lunch. Take a late afternoon
flight to Brisbane.

Suggested schedule

7:30	Breakfast at hotel; store your packed bags.
9:00*	Depart Cairns by rail for Kuranda.
10:30	Arrive Kuranda. Browse through the market, with plenty of time left to see sights of your choice and eat a bite of lunch.
1:30*	Depart Kuranda for Cairns.
3:00	Arrive Cairns. Return to your hotel, pick up your bags and head for the airport.
5:15	Depart Cairns on Ansett Flight 39 to Brisbane. Dinner en route
7:50	Arrive Brisbane. Check into hotel.

* Cairns – Kuranda schedule may vary slightly
by season.

Sightseeing highlights

● ● ● **The Cairns – Kuranda Railway** was an engineering
marvel of the late 19th century. Between 1886 and 1891, a team
of more than 1,500 labourers carved this 34-km (21-mile) narrow-
gauge track from the side of a mountain using pick, shovel and
dynamite. They installed 15 tunnels, 98 curves, and dozens of
bridges in the 1,055-foot climb from lush canefields up the
Barron River Gorge to Kuranda village on the edge of the
Atherton Tableland.

Today, tourists can make the same dramatic journey in colonial-
style railcars for a round-trip price of A$10.20 (£4.85). After
leaving Cairns (or the alternate restaurant-depot in suburban
Freshwater), the train climbs past Horseshoe Bend, with vast
views across the chessboard of canefields to the Coral Sea. (On
clear days, you can easily pick out Green Island on the Great
Barrier Reef.) After passing Stony Creek Falls, there are

breathtaking views of the precipitous Barron River Gorge wherever breaks in the dense rainforest vegetation allow. The train finally emerges at the great Barron Falls, a short distance from Kuranda.

● **Barron Falls** must have been magnificent before its powerful waters were harnessed by a major hydroelectric project. A small quantity of water is still allowed to trickle over the huge rock wall—more, of course, during the rainy season—to allow visitors to imagine the former grandeur of this great cataract. The train makes a photo stop at the Falls Lookout at the end of the Barron Falls Road from Kuranda. There's also a track from the lookout to the bottom of the gorge for hiking diehards.

● **Kuranda Railway Station** is a lovely relic of bygone days. Built in 1915, it is an oasis in the midst of a tropical jungle, and is itself a greenhouse of hanging ferns.

●● **Kuranda** (pop. 500) lives up to its billing as 'the village in the rainforest'. Its tree-lined main street, which leads about a half-mile from the station to the market, features numerous arts and crafts galleries and Devonshire tea shops. Horse-drawn carts ply the short route.

Wednesday and Sunday are market days in Kuranda. The open-air **Kuranda Market**, winding around a hill and across a small stream at the west end of town, gives local artisans and fruit growers a chance to sell their wares and produce. Here's where you'll find hand-painted T-shirts, leather goods, pottery and woodwork, as well as tropical delights like mangoes, starfruit and custard apples. The market is open rain or shine, April to October, Wednesdays 9:00 a.m. to noon and Sundays 9:00 a.m. to 1:00 p.m. Nearby is the small **Heritage Homestead** historical museum (admission A$3 (£1.40)).

Across the road from the market is the **Kuranda Wildlife Noctarium**, an indoor zoo with simulated forest conditions for nocturnal Australian fauna (admission A$4.50 (£2.15)). Also in Kuranda, you'll find the **Honey House**, where bees in glass hives produce honey sold behind the counter (free admission); the **Cape York Experience**, an audiovisual programme screening daily at Kuranda Village Centre (admission A$3.50 (£1.66)); and the **Jilli Binna Museum**, a display of artifacts from Aboriginal rainforest culture (admission 50 cents (24p)). The new **Australian Butterfly Farm**, just out of town, promises to be a major attraction. Back near the railway station, the *Kuranda Queen* departs hourly for a 50-minute riverboat cruise on the Barron River (fare A$6.50 (£3.10)).

Brisbane orientation

Queensland's capital, a city of 1.1 million people, sprawls for

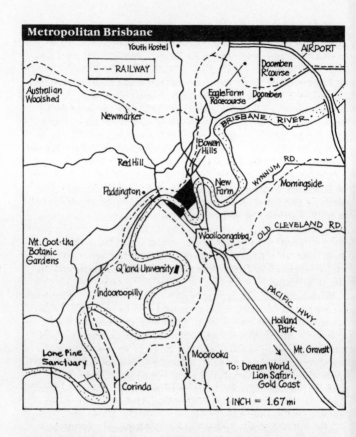

an amazing 471 square miles around both banks of the Brisbane River. (That makes it the third largest city in the world in area.) Its central core, however, is relatively small, swallowing up a single horseshoe bend some 30 km upriver from Moreton Bay.

Like several other Australian cities, Brisbane (pronounced 'Briz-b'n') got its start as a convict settlement. Agricultural and mining wealth from the vast inland reaches of the state made the city prosperous in the late 19th and early 20th centuries. Today Brisbane has blossomed into a progressive garden city.

The symbol of this newfound refinement is the Queensland Cultural Centre, a brilliant fine and performing arts complex on the banks of the river, across from the city centre.

Brisbane has a subtropical climate, with warm, rainy summers (temperatures range from 67 to 85 degrees Fahrenheit) and drier winters (49 to 69 degrees F).

Most of the main streets in central Brisbane have been named after British rulers, so if you know your history, this should come easy. From the direction of the airport, in northeast Brisbane, Ann Street is the principal thoroughfare leading into the centre. It skirts the central railway station and King George Square, essentially marking the northwestern edge of the city centre. Albert Street running at right angles to Ann Street through the Square, is the main northwest–southeast artery. Ann is paralleled to the southeast by Adelaide, Queen, Elizabeth, Charlotte, Mary, Margaret and Alice Streets, with the Botanic Gardens taking the southernmost chunk of the 'horse-shoe'. Albert is paralleled to the southwest by George and William Streets, and to the northeast by Edward, Creek and Wharf Streets. King George Square, on which sits the City Hall, and Queen Street between Albert and Edward are pedestrian arcades.

City transport

Skennars Transport (tel. 832-1148) provides shuttle-bus service to central Brisbane from the domestic and international airport terminals, a distance of some 10 km (6 miles). Buses run half-hourly, and the charge is A$2.70 (£1.30). (You can also catch a No. 160 city bus for 80 cents (38p).) Taxis charge about A$7 (£3.33) over the same distance. Several car-hire agencies have desks at the airport, but you probably won't need one for the remainder of your stay.

Within the city, Queensland Railways' electric Citytrain (tel. 225-0211) and City Council buses (tel. 225-4444) provide service to nearly all points. Six Citytrain lines extend some 45 km (28 miles) east–west from Shorncliffe to Ipswich, 75 km (45 miles) north–south from Caboolture to Beenleigh. Trains operate daily from approximately 4:30 a.m. to 1:30 a.m. (with limited hours on weekends). A one-segment fare is 60 cents (28p). Bus tickets are 50 cents (23p) for one zone, 80 cents (38p) for two, or you can buy a $3 (£1.40) Day Rover ticket providing unlimited bus transport for one day (5:30 a.m. to 11:30 p.m.). There's also a Brisbane River Ferry Service (tel. 399-4768) providing river crossings at several points for just 40 cents (19p). Brisbane Bicycle Hire, 214 Margaret Street (tel. 229-2592) has bicycles for hire at A$3.50 (£1.66) an hour or A$12 (£5.70) an 8-hour day

Where to stay

Brisbane is among the more expensive Australian cities for over-night stays, and it's not getting any cheaper. Its two newest hotels—the **Hilton International**, 190 Elizabeth Street (tel. 231-3131) and the **Sheraton Brisbane**, 249 Turbot Street (tel. 835-3535)—provide luxury world-class accommodation. The

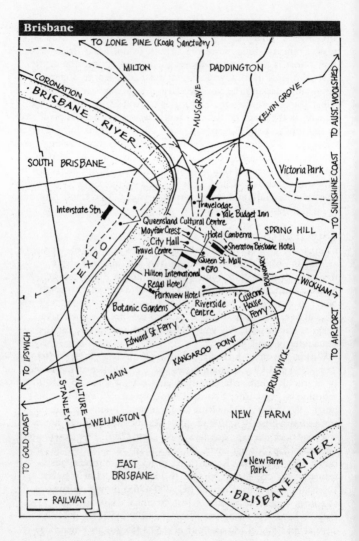

Brisbane

TO LONE PINE (Koala Sanctuary)

MILTON   PADDINGTON

CORONATION

BRISBANE RIVER

MUSGRAVE

KELVIN GROVE

TO AUST. WOOLSHED

SOUTH BRISBANE

Victoria Park

TO SUNSHINE COAST

Interstate Stn.

EXPO

• Travelodge
• Yale Budget Inn

Queensland Cultural Centre
Mayfair Crest   Hotel Canberra   SPRING HILL
City Hall   •Sheraton Brisbane Hotel
Travel Centre   Queen St. Mall
•Hilton International   • GPO
Regal Hotel
•Parkview Hotel
Botanic Gardens   Riverside   Customs
    Centre   House Ferry

BOUNDARY   WICKHAM

TO AIRPORT

Edward St. Ferry

KANGAROO POINT

TO IPSWICH

MAIN   BRUNSWICK

STANLEY   VULTURE

WELLINGTON   NEW FARM

TO GOLD COAST

EAST BRISBANE

• New Farm Park

BRISBANE RIVER

--- RAILWAY

Hilton features a 25-storey garden atrium, while the 441-room Sheraton looms directly above the central station. A small step down in price is the **Mayfair Crest**, a businessmen's favourite at Ann and Roma Streets, King George Square (tel. 229-9111).

The **Brisbane City Travelodge**, Roma Street near George Street (tel. 238-2222), is one of Brisbane's best bargains, with luxury-class facilities at moderate prices. Also centrally located and mid-priced are the **Bellevue Hotel**, 103 George Street (tel. 221-6044); the **Parkview Motel**, 128 Alice Street (tel. 31-2695); and the **Regal Motel**, 132 Alice Street (tel. 31-1541).

The **Yale Budget Inn**, 413 Upper Edward Street (tel. 832-1663), is a bed-and-breakfast guest house extremely popular among economy travellers. **Marrs Town House**, 391 Wickham Terrace (tel. 831-5388), is newer accommodation near Albert Park while the **Atcherly Hotel**, 513 Queen Street (tel. 832-2591), is an old standby. Budget travellers must book at the downtown YHA office, 462 Queen Street, before catching a No. 172 bus north to the **Brisbane Youth Hostel**, 15 Mitchell Street in Kedron (tel. 57-1245), 8 km north of the city centre. Much nearer town are the two independent **Brisbane Backpackers Inns** in New Farm, at 71 Kent Street (tel. 385-4504) and 365 Bowen Terrace (tel. 358-1488).

Where to eat

There are a number of good restaurants, as befits a city of this size.

The southeast Queensland coast is renowned for its seafood—particularly the Moreton Bay bugs (a lobster relation) and the Queensland mud crabs. You can't go wrong ordering them at **Gambaro's**, a casual cafe just west of the centre at 34 Caxton Street, Petrie Terrace, or the **Breakfast Creek Wharf**, east of the central city at 160 Breakfast Creek Road, Newstead. In the centre, **Conia's**, 132 Albert Street, has excellent seafood.

In the central city area, the best upmarket dining is in the best hotels. **Michael's Riverside**, in the new Riverside Centre at 123 Eagle Street, wins plaudits for its French cuisine. But many casual, less expensive spots are fun, too—like **Jimmy's on the Mall**, a licensed open-air restaurant in the Queen Street Mall. In the Elizabeth Arcade off Charlotte Street, **Tortilla** (Aussies pronounce the 'L's) is an atmospheric choice for decent Mexican food and **The Source** has good, cheap vegetarian offerings. **Mama Luigi's**, 240 St Paul's Terrace, is a long-standing Italian favourite, and you can eat like a Russian at **Czars**, 47 Elizabeth Street.

The adjacent suburbs of Fortitude Valley and New Farm, walking distance east of the centre (via Ann Street or Wickham Street), feature many authentic low-priced ethnic restaurants. Try **Giardinetto's** (Italian), 336 Brunswick Street; **Cathay** (Chinese), 222 Wickham Street; **Baan Thai** (Thai), 630 Brunswick Street; and **Possum's** (fair dinkum Aussie), 681 Brunswick Street. Further toward the airport, the **Breakfast Creek Hotel**, 2 Kingsford Smith Drive, has a nationally famous steak-and-beer garden.

In Petrie Terrace, **Rag's**, 25 Caxton Street, has a reputation as Brisbane's best French restaurant. The **Caxton Garden Grill**, in the Caxton Hotel, provides jazz accompaniment to meals. In nearby Paddington, the **Elephant Bath**, 183 Given Terrace, offers a rare Asian delight: Sri Lankan curries.

Nightlife

The **Performing Arts Complex**, in the aforementioned Queensland Cultural Centre, comprises the Concert Hall for symphonic performances, the Lyric Theatre for opera, ballet, drama and musical comedy, and the Cremorne Theatre for smaller and experimental productions. Almost any major performance will be presented here. Events schedules can be obtained, and bookings made, by calling 844-0201 or visiting the PAC box office. The Cultural Centre is on the south side of the Brisbane River at Grey and Melbourne Streets.

Other good spots for live theatre include the **S.G.I.O. Theatre**, Turbot and Albert Streets, home of the Queensland Theatre Company, and **La Boite**, 57 Hale Street in Milton, home of the Brisbane Repertory Company. Queensland film censors are more protective of viewers than other states, but you'll find a good number of cinemas in the central area, especially on Albert Street.

Brisbane's most popular disco-nightclubs, at the time of writing, were **Sibyl's**, 383 Adelaide Street, with three floors of dancing and entertainment; and the **Brisbane Underground**, Caxton and Hal Streets in Paddington. Both are open until 3:00 a.m. Wednesdays to Saturdays. The major hotels all have their posh nightspots.

For live music, try the **Hacienda Hotel**, Brunswick and McLachlan Streets in Fortitude Valley, for rock; the **Blue Moon Cafe**, 540 Queen Street, for jazz; or the **Treasury Hotel**, Elizabeth and George Streets, for blues. **Wilson's 1870**, 103 Queen Street, appeals to an older crowd with a piano bar and cocktail music.

Helpful hints

The Brisbane Visitors and Convention Bureau (tel. 221-8411), in City Hall on the west side of King George Square, is open weekdays 8:30 a.m. to 5:00 p.m. The Queensland Government Travel Centre is at 196 Adelaide Street (tel. 31-2211), open 9:00 a.m. to 4:45 p.m. Monday to Friday, 9:00 to 11:15 a.m. Saturday. There are tourist information booths in the Queen Street Mall and the Brisbane Transit Centre on Roma Street.

In case of emergencies, dial 000. There's also a 24-hour number for medical service: 378-6900.

TOUR 20

BRISBANE AND THE GOLD COAST

Your time is limited, so it's a good day to see the sights from a
city tour bus. Be sure the itinerary includes the Lone Pine Koala
Sanctuary: if you ever wanted a photo of yourself holding one of
these seemingly cuddly creatures, here's where to have it taken.
After lunch, take a bus to the Gold Coast. Catch the day's last
rays on the beach.

Suggested schedule

8:00	Breakfast at hotel.
9:00	Half-day morning tour of city, including the Lone Pine Koala Sanctuary, Mount Coot-tha Gardens and the Queensland Cultural Centre.
12:30	Return from tour. Lunch.
2:00	Board a bus for the Gold Coast.
3:30	Arrive at Surfers Paradise. Check into hotel.
4:30	Hit the beach.
6:30	Relax at hotel.
7:30	Dinner
9:00	Go out on the town.

Brisbane sightseeing highlights
● ● **City tours** are something I'm not normally crazy about—
mainly because I prefer to explore a new place in my own time—
but given the limited time allotted to Brisbane in this itinerary, a
bus tour is the most efficient way to see the main attractions.
Ansett Pioneer Tours (tel. 226-1184) show off the city sights in a
half-day tour leaving major hotels at 9:00 a.m. daily (fare A\$12
(£5.70)); Aladdin's Magic Carpet Tours (tel. 345-8300) start just
15 minutes later (fare A\$14 (£6.66)). Both 'Beautiful Brisbane'
tours last 3½ hours. Boomerang Tours' (tel. 221-9922) three-hour
'Morning City Sights' tour (fare A\$10 (£4.75)) starts at 10:00 a.m.
Saturday, Sunday and Monday only.
● ● ● **Lone Pine Koala Sanctuary**, on the banks of the
Brisbane River off Jesmond Road in Fig Tree Pocket, 11 km (7
miles) from the city centre, has more koalas (over 100) than any
other wildlife reserve in Australia. You can have your photo taken
cuddling one of the creatures (beware the sharp claws), visit the
maternity wing and see newborn koalas, and feed the freely

roaming kangaroos and emus. There are a variety of other
Australian animals, birds and reptiles in the park as well. Open
daily 9:30 a.m. to 5:00 p.m. Adult admission is A$6.50 (£3.10).

You can reach the Lone Pine Sanctuary on your own by taking
a No. 84 bus from Adelaide Street. A better way to arrive, if
you've got an afternoon free, is to join the Koala Cruise (tel.
229-7055) leaving daily at 1:15 p.m. from Queens Wharf Road,
North Quay (near the centre). The cruise costs A$9 (£4.25);
combined with a return coach tour, it's A$14 (£6.66).

● **Mount Coot-tha Botanic Gardens**, Toowong, feature native
and imported plants in the tropical rainforest, sub-tropical and
desert settings. They're open daily 7:00 a.m. to 5:00 p.m. The Sir
Thomas Brisbane Planetarium offers a star-gazing show from
Wednesday to Sunday between noon and 7:00 p.m.; bookings are
essential. Atop Mount Coot-tha, just 8 km (5 miles) from the city
centre, is a restaurant with panoramic views all the way to
Moreton Bay. Other major gardens in Brisbane include the City
Botanic Gardens, at the south end of Albert Street; New Farm
Park, east of the centre off Brunswick Street; and Newstead Park
on Breakfast Creek Road, harbouring Brisbane's oldest building,
the 1846 Newstead House.

●● **The Queensland Cultural Centre** occupies a 14.7-acre site
on the south bank of the Brisbane River, facing the city centre
across the Victoria Bridge. A series of distinctive white structures
set amid landscaped gardens, sculptures and water malls, this
A$173 million (£82.4 million) complex has four components: the
Queensland Art Gallery (opened in 1982), the Performing Arts
Complex (1985), the Queensland Museum (1986), and the State
Library (1988). A convention centre, three restaurants, four
cafeterias and several speciality shops are among its facilities. The
Queensland Cultural Centre Trust (tel. 240-7229) has full infor-
mation.

The Queensland Art Gallery (tel. 240-7333) displays its
permanent collection of Australian and European art, plus
numerous touring shows, in 15 separate exhibition areas. A wide
variety of lectures, workshops and musical performances are
regularly offered. There's free admission to the gallery, open daily
10:00 a.m. to 5:00 p.m., Wednesday to 8:00 p.m. Guided tours
are available weekdays at 11:00 a.m., 1:00 and 2:00 p.m., and
weekends at 2:00 and 3:00 p.m., for no additional charge. The
125-year-old **Queensland Museum** (tel. 240-7633) has three
floors of displays emphasising the state's geology and natural
history, Aboriginal roots and Melanesian influences, pioneer
history and early technology. Popular with children is a large
outdoor Dinosaur Garden. Open daily 9:00 a.m. to 5:00 p.m.,
Wednesday to 8:00 p.m. Admission is free.

The Performing Arts Complex (tel. 240-7483) attracted nearly 1 million patrons to its three theatres during its first two years of operation (see 'Nightlife', Tour 19). Performers included the Royal Shakespeare Company, the Bolshoi Ballet and the London Philharmonic Orchestra. Guided tours are offered hourly, 10:00 a.m. to 4:00 p.m., Monday to Saturday, for A$2.50 (£1.20). These are backstage tours on selected days by reservation for A$5 (£2.40).

● **The Australian Woolshed**, 15 km (9½ miles) from the centre at 148 Samford Road, Ferny Hills, is as close as you're likely to get to an authentic Aussie sheep station in a metropolitan area. Working sheepdogs demonstrate their skill, and there are exhibits of wool classing and spinning. There's no admission charge to the complex, open daily 9:30 a.m. to 6:00 p.m., but if you want to see the shearing demonstration and parade of trained rams at 10:45 a.m. daily or 2:00 p.m. Sunday, you'll have to pay A$4.50 (£2.15). The craft shop has been voted Australia's best. A licensed Outback-style restaurant features 'bush dances' on Friday and Saturday from 7:00 p.m. to midnight.

●**Earlystreet Historical Village**, 75 McIlwraith Avenue, Norman Park, is a collection of eight historic Queensland buildings set in five acres of colonial gardens surrounding the 19th century Eulalia Manor. You'll find an old slab hut, a shearers' pub, a general store, a blacksmith's shop, a coach house and several residences, all relocated to this site and refurnished in mid-1800s style. Classified by the National Trust, the village is open weekdays 9:30 a.m. to 4:30 p.m., Saturday and Sunday from 10:30 a.m. Admission is A$4 (£1.90).

● **The Kookaburra Queen** is an elegant wooden paddlewheeler that plies the waters of the Brisbane River several times daily. Ninety-minute tea or snack cruises, leaving at 10:00 a.m. (daily except Saturday), 12:45 p.m. (weekdays) and 3:00 p.m. (Sundays), cost just A$10.90 (£5.20). Daily dinner cruises, boarding at 7:00 p.m., are priced from A$27.90 to A$34.90 (£13.25 to £16.60). The Queen leaves from the Petrie Bight Marina on Howard Street, at the east end of the city near the National Hotel.

The Paddington Circle is the quaintest shopping area in Brisbane. Merchants have retained and restored the suburb's original colonial architecture to give the whole district a heritage feeling. Most of the shops are along Given Terrace and Latrobe Terrace.

Getting to the Gold Coast

Except in the middle of the night, you'll never have to wait longer than an hour or two to catch a bus from Brisbane to Australia's favourite beach resort. Greyhound buses (tel.

240-9333) leave at least 10 times a day from the Roma Street
Transit Centre. Skennars Transport (tel. 832-1148) also has
several buses departing daily for the Gold Coast from its depot on
Barry Parade near Fortitude Valley. The fare is A$8.10 (£3.80),
whether you head for Southport (1 hour 15 minutes), Surfers
Paradise (1½ hours) or Coolangatta (about two hours).

There is soon to be a rail link between Brisbane and the Gold
Coast.

Gold Coast orientation

A glittering white-sand beach stretching 32 km (20 miles) down
the coast of southeasternmost Queensland, just 65 km (40 miles)
from Brisbane, the Gold Coast is the single most popular resort
strip in Australia. That has both good and bad connotations.
There are hotels, restaurants and nightspots of all standards and
prices, a lush mountain backdrop not far from the lovely beach,
and an incredible variety of man-made attractions. But there's also
a great deal of crass commercialism and tourist kitsch preying on
the throngs in transition. Overlook that and you'll have a great
time.

At least a dozen separate communities, linked by the busy Gold
Coast Highway, comprise the City of Gold Coast. About 200,000
people make their home along this narrow strip, four times the
population of 20 years ago. Southport, the Gold Coast's northernmost community, is its commercial and industrial centre. Surfers
Paradise, the next main centre reached heading south, is the
Marbella-style high-rise capital of the coast, and the site of its
most frenetic nightlife. Halfway down the coast is Burleigh
Heads, a laid-back family community at the foot of fauna-rich
Burleigh Heads National Park. Coolangatta marks not only the
southern extreme of the Gold Coast, but also the boundary
between Queensland and New South Wales. The Gold Coast
Airport, with direct links to Sydney, Melbourne, Adelaide and
other cities, is here.

Local transport

Don't worry about being stuck on the Gold Coast without a car.
You can either base yourself in one town and cope quite nicely,
or you can call upon Surfside buses (tel. 36-2449) for regular
transport links between Southport and Coolangatta. No fare is
higher than A$2 (95p). Smekels Busline (tel. 32-6211) serves the
Southport area more thoroughly, but doesn't go further south
than Broadbeach. Silly Style, 6 Beach Road, Surfers, will rent you
a bike or moped.

Where to stay

As Surfers Paradise (usually called 'Surfers') is the centre of most
of the action, we'll deal with it first. At the top of the line are
the elegant **Ramada At Paradise Centre**, Gold Coast Highway
and Hanlan Street (tel. 075/59-34000) and the **Holiday Inn-
Surfers Paradise**, 22 View Street (tel. 59-1000). The **Chevron
Paradise Hotel**, Ferny Avenue (tel. 39-0444), is a good choice in
the moderate price bracket. You're reaching a bit to find a decent
economy room in Surfers, but the **Hub Motel**, 21 Cavill Avenue
(tel. 31-5559) will do quite nicely. The nearest budget
accommodation to Surfers is the AYH hostel in the **El Dorado
Motel**, 2821 Gold Coast Highway (tel. 31-5155), nearly a mile
south of Surfers. You must check in between 4:00 and 6:00 p.m.

Outside of Surfers, the best accommodation is the **Conrad
International Hotel**, Gold Coast Highway, Broadbeach Island
(tel. 92-1133). It's the site of Jupiter's Casino. You'll find
moderate and economy-priced motels all along the Gold Coast
Highway from here south, but Coolangatta is the king in these
price ranges. Try the **Pacific Village Hotel**, 88 Marine Parade
(tel. 36-2733), or the **Bombora Holiday Lodge**, Marine Parade
at Dutton Street (tel. 36-1888). The **Backpackers Inn**, 45
McLean Street, Coolangatta (tel. 36-2422), costs less than A$8
(£3.80) a night and has a licensed restaurant and bar on the
premises.

Where to eat

There are as many different kinds of places to eat on the Gold
Coast as there are kinds of people who visit, and that's a lot. The
coast's characterisation as a utopia for junk-food junkies is not
totally inaccurate, but there is no shortage of more wholesome
dining establishments.

In Surfers, try the **Rusty Pelican,** Orchid and Elkhorn
Avenues, or the **Captain's Tale**, 5 Cavill Avenue on the arcade,
for seafood; **Pellegrini**, 3120 Gold Coast Highway, for Italian
cuisine; or **Shogun**, 90 Bundall Road, for Japanese food. Be
warned, however: none of them is cheap. You can spend less
money and have a lot of fun at the hofbrau-style **Bavarian Steak
House**, Gold Coast Highway at Cavill Avenue; the **Tandoori
Taj** (North Indian), 3100 Gold Coast Highway; the **Mexican
Kitchen,** 150 Bundall Road; or the **Athens** (Greek), Gold Coast
Highway near Laycock Street. The **Surfer's Deli**, 25 Orchid
Avenue, is a pleasant sidewalk café with light meals and
entertainment.

Up and down the coast the **Holy Mackerel**, 174 Marine
Parade, Labrador (north of Southport), offers free shuttle service
from Surfers to its seafood restaurant. Mermaid Beach has a good

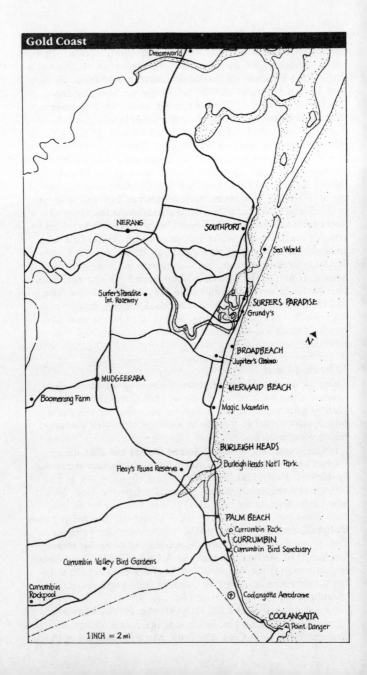

Gold Coast

Dreamworld

NERANG   SOUTHPORT

Sea World

Surfer's Paradise
Int. Raceway

SURFERS PARADISE
Grundy's

N

BROADBEACH
Jupiter's Casino

MUDGEERABA   MERMAID BEACH

Boomerang Farm   Magic Mountain

BURLEIGH HEADS

Fleay's Fauna Reserve   Burleigh Heads Nat'l Park

PALM BEACH
Currumbin Rock
CURRUMBIN
Currumbin Bird Sanctuary

Currumbin Valley Bird Gardens

Currumbin
Rockpool

Coolangatta Aerodrome

COOLANGATTA
Point Danger

1 INCH = 2 mi

Italian restaurant, **Gino's Osteria**, 2563 Gold Coast Highway,
and nearby on the same road, the most passionately named
vegetarian eatery I've ever heard of—the **Lusty Lentil**.

Further down, in Burleigh Heads, the **Chieng Mai Thai**
restaurant is at 31 James Street. Finally, no south end budget
watcher should pass up a $3.30 (£1.60) counter meal at the
Queensland Hotel, Boundary Street, Coolangatta.

Nightlife

The cards are dealt 24 hours a day at **Jupiter's Casino** in the
Conrad International Hotel on Broadbeach Island. Blackjack,
roulette, craps, baccarat, keno, and several other games are played
continuously in this sophisticated new casino. There are also
several restaurants and a showroom featuring world-class
entertainers.

In Surfers, the overloaded disco-cabaret lineup includes such
highlights as **Twains International** and the five-storey **Pent-
house**, both on Orchid Avenue. The **Swingin' Vine**, 47A Cavill
Avenue, is noted for jazz and comedy. Ask for directions to **Bom-
bay Rock**, the best of several clubs in Surfers that feature live
rock. Its counterpart, 13 km (8 miles) south of Surfers in North
Palm Beach, is the **Playroom**, on the Gold Coast Highway
opposite the Tallebudgera Bridge.

There's cheaper entertainment just across the New South Wales
border from Coolangatta, in the town of Tweed Heads. The club
scene flourishes here where poker machines ('one-armed bandits')
are legal. Meals, drinks and top-flight entertainment are always
reduced in price to entice you to play the machines. They're
technically membership clubs, but out-of-state visitors, especially
foreigners, are welcomed. Shuttle buses can run you from Surfers
or elsewhere on the Gold Coast to such spots as **Twin Towns
Services Club**, Wharf Street; **Tweed Heads Bowls Club**,
Tweed Street; and my favourite, **Seagulls Rugby League
Football Club**, Gollan Drive.

For romancers or real budget watchers, there's nothing cheaper
than a walk on a moonlit beach.

Helpful hints

The Gold Coast Visitors and Convention Bureau has its main
offices in the Cavill Mall, Surfers Paradise (tel. 38-4419). (There's
a Coolangatta branch: tel. 26-7765.) You'll also find the Queensland Government Travel Centre here on the second floor of the
TAA Building, 38–40 Cavill Avenue (tel. 92-1033). All are open
9:00 a.m. to 4:45 p.m. weekdays, 9:00 to 11:15 a.m. Saturday.

The Surfers Paradise post office is at the corner of Cavill
Avenue and the Gold Coast Highway. Banking hours are 9:30

a.m. to 4:00 p.m. Monday to Thursday, to 5:00 p.m. Friday.
Retail shops are open daily except Sunday, 9:00 a.m. to 5:30 p.m.
   In case of emergencies, dial 000. For 24-hour medical
assistance, call 38 – 8823.

TOUR 21

THE GOLD COAST

Your final day on Australian beaches. Why not decide for
yourself if the name 'Surfers Paradise' really fits? Or head for the
tourist attractions like Sea World, the Currumbin Bird Sanctuary
or the Mudgeeraba Boomerang Farm.

Suggested schedule	
7:30	Up and at 'em, unless you need extra sleep to recover from last night's fling.
9:00	Visit the Currumbin Sanctuary near Palm Beach.
11:00	Catch a few late morning rays.
12:30	Lunch
1:30	Sea World is worth a full afternoon.
5:00	Head back to your hotel. Take a quick dip in the pool.
6:30	Dinner
8:00	It's your last night in Australia—what you do with it is up to you.

Sightseeing highlights
● ● **The Currumbin Sanctuary**, just off the Gold Coast
Highway on Tomewin Street, Currumbin, 18 km (11 miles) south
of Surfers, is a tourist favourite mainly because of the flocks of
brightly coloured rainbow lorikeets which fly in daily from their
homes in the wild to be fed from plates of honey by willing
visitors. Arrive before 10:00 a.m. to see the mass of orange-
breasted, blue-headed, green-backed birds, or wait until about 4:00
in the afternoon. A variety of other native birds, koalas, kangaroos
and wallabies make their homes in the 50-acre wildlife refuge.
You can walk among the creatures or watch from a 2-km
miniature railway. Numerous craftsmen ply their trades; among
them are potters, glass blowers and gem cutters. Open daily 8:00
a.m. to 5:00 p.m. Adult admission is A$8 (£3.80).
● ● **Sea World,** on the Spit 5 km (3 miles) north of Surfers, is
Australia's No. 1 marine theme park. Dolphins, killer whales and
sea lions alternately awe and amuse audiences in separate shows,
as do acrobatic water skiers. The World of the Sea Theatre
combines audiovisuals with live demonstrations of underwater
diving and shark feeding. Visitors can pet dolphins, feed sea lions

and gaze at an enormous aquarium. The park's dozen rides include Australia's first free-fall waterslide (with a frightening five-storey drop!) and its only triple-loop roller-coaster, as well as a monorail and carousel for those of less intestinal fortitude.

Sea World is open daily (except Christmas) from 10:00 a.m. to 5:00 p.m. The adult admission of A$18 (£8.50) includes all rides and performances. Call 32–1055 or 32–5131 (recorded) for daily show times and bus connections.

Dreamworld, in Coomera, 15 minutes toward Brisbane from Surfers, is Australia's largest Disney-style theme park. This 208-acre complex has a little of everything. You can see the Koala Country Music Show, for example, with 22 life-size but computerised Aussie animals doing the singing and playing. You can take any of 17 different rides, among them a steam train, a 'Murrissippi River' cruise and a high-speed trip through Avalanche Mountain. Seventeen shops and 11 restaurants take care of shopping and hunger pangs.

Dreamworld is open Saturday to Wednesday, 10:00 a.m. to 5:00 p.m., daily during school holiday periods. Adult admission of A$15 (£7.15) includes all rides and performances. Round-trip express bus service from the Gold Coast is offered for A$6 (£2.85) by Keith's Tours (tel. 30–5908).

Magic Mountain, on the Gold Coast Highway at Nobby's Beach near Miami, is another man-made attraction of the same ilk. You can't miss seeing the medieval castle atop the bluff long before you arrive. The numerous rides include a chairlift to carry you to the mountaintop for panoramic views of the Gold Coast. But the highlight of a visit is 'Visions', a superb show presented by magician and illusionist Arthur Coghlan. Open Sunday to Thursday, 10:00 a.m. to 5:00 p.m., daily in summer and during school holiday periods. Adult admission of A$10.50 (£5) includes all rides and shows. Call 52–2333 to arrange free bus pickup from hotels.

Burleigh Heads National Park is a small, unexpected natural bushland oasis in the middle of this utterly commercial area. Koalas, wallabies, bandicoots and much birdlife inhabit this bluff overlooking the mouth of Tallebudgera Creek. A graded 3-km (2-mile) walking track leads around the headland.

Mudgeeraba Boomerang Farm, on Springbrook Road, 20 minutes inland from the Gold Coast, is not a major tourist attraction. Unlike others, however, it's uniquely Australian. Not only will the Hawes family sell you a boomerang made in their own factory; they'll teach you how to throw it so that it comes back to you. Their 200-acre farm also has a fascinating boomerang museum. Open seven days a week. Ask directions locally or phone 30–5231.

● **Lamington National Park** comprises some 50,000 acres of
lushly forested mountains 43 km (27 miles) from the Gold Coast
via Nerang. Some call it 'the Green behind the Gold'. The park
contains 140 km (87 miles) of walking tracks, an estimated 500
waterfalls, and a forest of 3,000-year-old beech trees. Two small
guest houses, at Binna Burra and O'Reilly's, serve park visitors.
Grundy's at Paradise Centre is the sort of place that shoppers
and fun-seekers don't need to be told about: they'll find it on
their own. Set dead centre in Surfers Paradise, with direct access
from the beach, Ramada Hotel or Cavill Mall, this three-storey
complex includes 110 boutiques and speciality shops, an
international food village, and the most cacophonous collection of
video games you've ever heard (or seen).
Pacific Fair, near the casino-hotel in Broadbeach, is the Gold
Coast's other most interesting shopping centre. The architects
have recreated streets from all over the world—from Oxford Street
(London) to the Boulevarde St Michel (Paris), Basin Street (New
Orleans) to Lindenstrasse (Berlin). Appropriate speciality shops
intermingle with chain department stores.

TOUR 22

FLY HOME FROM BRISBANE

It's been a great trip. Start your flight home in Brisbane.

Farewell advice

You should call your airline a couple of days early to confirm
your departure date and time.

The buses of Skennars Transport (tel. 38–9444 in Surfers,
36–2574 in Coolangatta) offer direct shuttle service from the
Gold Coast to Brisbane International Airport. The fare is A$8.10
(£3.85). Remember to allow 1½ hours for the trip from Surfers,
two hours from Coolangatta.

When you reach Brisbane, tell the driver if you need the
international terminal. The domestic terminal, where you arrived,
is a considerable drive away, around the runways.

Don't spend all your money before reaching the airport. You'll
have to hold on to A$20 (£9.50) to pay the airport departure tax.

As you head back home you can think back on a great
holiday—and where you want to go on your next trip Down
Under.

POST TOUR OPTIONS

The biggest frustration in trying to cover an entire continent in a short holiday is omitting so many worthwhile spots from the itinerary. If you've got the time, the following five options can be spliced into your schedule as follows:

Tasmania—Leave from and return to Melbourne (Tour 8).

Adelaide and/or **Perth**—Between Melbourne and Alice Springs (Tour 11).

Darwin—Between Alice Springs and Cairns (Tour 16).

Barrier Reef Islands—Between Cairns and Brisbane (Tour 19).

TASMANIA

Australia's island state, some 230 km (143 miles) across Bass Strait from Victoria, is almost a world unto itself, its colonial manors scattered through the lowlands beneath forested mountain peaks.

Suggested 6-day schedule	
DAY 1	Arrive in Devonport from Melbourne. Hire a car and drive to Launceston.
DAY 2	See Cataract Gorge, then drive down the east coast via Campbelltown to Port Arthur.
DAY 3	After exploring the former penal colony in the morning, drive to Hobart via Richmond.
DAY 4	Catch the view from Mount Wellington, then drive via Lake St Clair and Queenstown to Strahan.
DAY 5	Go on the Gordon River cruise in the morning, then drive to Stanley for the night.
DAY 6	Potter down the north coast to Devonport. Night flight or ferry voyage back to Melbourne.

Getting there

Two to five flights daily cross the Bass Strait between Melbourne and Hobart (the state capital), Launceston, Devonport, and Burnie/Wynyard. The flight takes 65 minutes to Hobart, 55 minutes to Launceston, 50 minutes to the other two north coast towns. The lowest round-trip fares, at the time of writing, were A$192 (£91.50) to Hobart, A$165 (£78.50) to Launceston, A$146

(£69.50) to Devonport and Burnie/Wynyard, on a 30-day advance purchase excursion basis. (If you're under 25, **East-West Airlines** will give you a 20% discount.) There are also direct flights several times a week to Launceston and Hobart from Sydney and the Gold Coast.

An overnight ferry, the *Abel Tasman*, crosses the strait three times a week, leaving Melbourne at 6 p.m. Monday, Wednesday and Friday and arriving in Devonport at 8:30 the following morning. Return boats leave Devonport at 6 p.m. Tuesday, Thursday and Sunday. One-way fares vary according to season and facilities, but range from A$75 (£35.75) in winter to A$109 (£52) in summer on the low end to A$141 to A$197 (£67 to £94) at the high end.

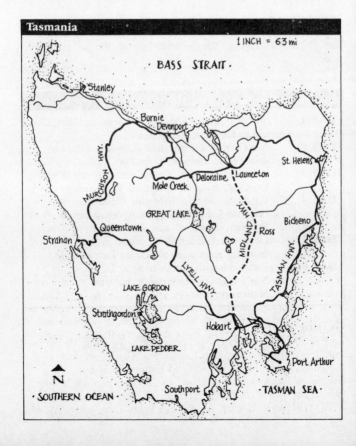

Tasmania

1 INCH = 63 mi

Getting around

The large car rental firms—Hertz, Avis and Budget—are
represented in all large towns in Tasmania. Weekly rates,
including unlimited kilometres, are similar, ranging from A$282
to A$600 (£134 to £286) depending upon class of vehicle. You'll
get a better deal from **Advance Travel Car Rentals** in
Devonport (tel. 004/24–8885) or Launceston (tel. 003–44–2164),
with weekly rates starting at A$144 (£68.50).

If you're a solo budget traveller, look into the seven-day 'Tassie
Pass' with **Tasmanian Redline Coaches** for A$60 (£28.50). (A
14-day pass is only A$75 (£35.75).) Book through Tasbureau (see
'Helpful Hints'). The Redline terminal to Devonport is at 9
Edward Street (tel. 004/24–2585); in Launceston at 112 George
Street (tel. 003/31–9177); in Hobart at 96 Harrington Street (tel.
004/34–4577).

Sightseeing highlights

● **Devonport**—(Pop. 25,000) is the market centre of the fertile
north coast region. **Tiagarra,** atop the headland called Mersey
Bluff, remembers the culture of the Tasmanian Aboriginal, one of
the most tragic races in history. Early settlers hunted down and
shot the native Tasmanians until a mere handful survived. They
were resettled off Tasmania's north coast, on Flinders Island,
where the last one died in 1876. Also in Devonport are the **Don
River Railway Museum**, the **Maritime Museum**, and
Taswegia historic printing and craft gallery.

● **Launceston**—Is Tasmania's second city, both in population
(65,000) and age (founded in 1805, a year after Hobart). Situated
at the head of the tranquil Tamar River, it is noted for its many
parks and gardens, especially **Cataract Gorge**. It is surrounded
by a rhododendron garden and crossed by an aerial chairlift. Also
see the **Queen Victoria Museum and Art Gallery** and the
Waverly Woollen Mills (tours daily 9 a.m. to 4 p.m.). Thirteen
km (8 miles) west of Launceston, near Hadspen, is the beautiful
Entally House historic homestead, built in 1819.

●●● **Port Arthur**—Was a name synonymous with harsh justice
in Australia's convict past. Between 1830 and 1877, some 12,500
hardened criminals lived in this isolated location under the threat
of the lash and long-term solitary isolation that drove many to
madness. Today, the restored **Port Arthur National Historic
Site** commemorates the nation's roots like nowhere else.

Elsewhere on the Tasman Peninsula, you can see spectacular
coastal formations—arches, undersea caves and blowholes—that
helped make this prison colony so difficult to escape from. **The
Bush Mill** theme park, 5 km (3 miles) north of the historic site,
recalls the days of the early timber cutters. The **Tasmanian**

Devil Park at Taranna, another 5 km north, is a good place to
see these varmints.

●● **Richmond**—Is a detour off the road back to Hobart, just 26
km (16 miles) northeast of the capital. The treasures of this
charming 1820s town include Australia's first bridge and its oldest
Catholic church. The Richmond Gaol has been faithfully
restored. Many of the community's elegant sandstone buildings
now house Devonshire tea shops, arts and crafts galleries and
historical museums.

●●● **Hobart**—Tasmania's capital and largest city (pop. 175,000)
was established in 1804 as the second European settlement in
Australia. The inner-city suburb of **Battery Point** is the original
seamen's quarter, where tiny cottages share the narrow winding
streets with Georgian mansions and Victorian terrace houses—
now, as often as not, occupied by restaurants, bed-and-breakfasts,
art galleries and antique shops. **The Van Diemen's Land
Memorial Folk Museum** in the Narryna mansion at 103
Hampden Road has a superb period collection. The **Maritime
Museum of Tasmania** in the Secheron House mansion off
Colville Street is also interesting.

Elsewhere in Hobart, see the excellent **Tasmanian Museum
and Art Gallery**, the **Royal Tasmanian Botanical Gardens**
and the scale-model **Tudor Court** at Sandy Bay. From the
summit of 4,170-foot **Mount Wellington**, a 20-km (12½-mile)
drive from the city centre, you can savour the spectacular layout
of this beautiful harbour city at the mouth of the Derwent River.

●● **Strahan**—A tiny fishing and timber port, is best known as
the starting point for cruises through Macquarie Harbour and up
the Gordon River, a crystalline stream that winds through
unexplored rainforest from **South West National Park**. Mount
Everest conqueror Sir Edmund Hillary has called this region 'the
greatest walking country in the world'. Some believe its denizens
may include the legendary Tasmanian wolf, a striped marsupial
canine last confirmed alive in the 1930s.

● **Stanley**—Has changed little since it was established in 1826 by
sheep breeders. Its combination of history and maritime beauty is
accented by **The Nut**, a striking 500-foot basalt outcropping that
dominates coastal scenery for many miles around.

● **The Northwest Coast** drive—129 km (80 miles) along the
Bass Highway from Stanley to Devonport, provides a final day of
Tasmanian wanderings. **Rocky Cape National Park** contains
Aboriginal caves, fields of wild orchids, and the glistening white-
sand **Sisters Beach** with Birdland Native Gardens reserve.
Lapoinya rhododendron gardens are nearby. At **Wynyard**, you'll
find **Fossil Bluff**, where the oldest marsupial fossil in Australia
was discovered. **Burnie** (pop. 21,000) has a major timber

products industry and the **Pioneer Village Museum**, recreating the town's turn-of-the-century commercial centre. Proceed east to the town of **Penguin**, which takes its name from colonies of fairy penguins living along the shore; **Ulverstone**, gateway to the Leven Canyon; and finally to **Devonport** and the Abel Tasman ferry terminal.

Helpful hints

Tasmania calls its state tourist agency **Tasbureau**. The head office is at 80 Elizabeth Street, Hobart (tel. 002-30-0211), but you'll find other offices along the route in Devonport (18 Rooke Street, tel. 004/24-1526); Launceston (St John and Paterson Streets, tel. 003/32-2101); Queenstown (39 Orr Street, tel. 004/71-1009); and Burnie (48 Cattley Street, tel. 004/30-2224). Most of these offices are open from 8:45 a.m. to 5:45 p.m. weekdays, 9 to 11 a.m. Saturdays.

In Melbourne, Tasbureau is at 256 Collins Street (tel. 03/63-6351) and in Sydney, at 129 King Street (tel. 02/233-2500). In the UK write to the Australian Tourist Commission, 4th Floor, Heathcote House, 20 Savile Row, London W1X 1AE (tel. 01-434 4372).

Two publications produced by Tasbureau are invaluable. *The Visitor's Guide to Tasmania* will tell you about every tourist attraction in the state. The bimonthly *Tasmanian Travelways* newspaper tells you how to get there, where to stay and where to eat, and how much it will cost you.

ADELAIDE AND SOUTH AUSTRALIA

South Australia calls itself the 'WOW' state—wine, opals and wildlife. The Barossa Valley northeast of Adelaide is Australia's premier wine-producing district; Coober Pedy, in the state's scorching outback, is the best-known opal-mining centre; and Kangaroo Island, off the south coast, may have a richer concentration of native fauna than any other part of the nation.

Adelaide, the pleasant capital of South Australia, is a perfect staging point for reaching these and other outlying attractions. Though Adelaide, with few points of major tourist interest, may come across to visitors as 'a big country town', its urban population of 900,000 is two-thirds that of the entire state. The city centre is lovely, carefully laid out beside the River Torrens and completely surrounded by a ring of spacious parkland.

I won't suggest a schedule here, since South Australia's attractions are in various directions from Adelaide and may not be practical to include in one itinerary without considerable time and/or money. Pick and choose spots that grab your interest.

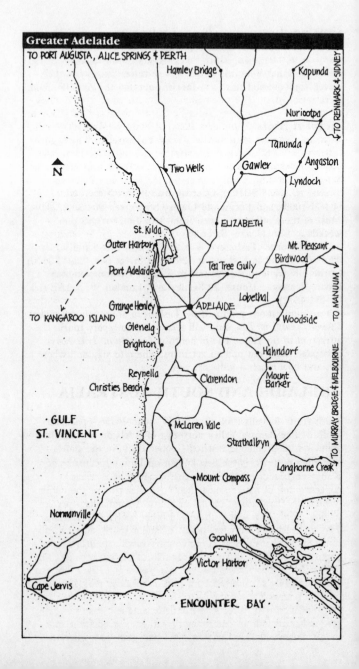

Greater Adelaide

TO PORT AUGUSTA, ALICE SPRINGS & PERTH
TO RENMARK & SIDNEY

Hamley Bridge
Kapunda
Nuriootpa
Tanunda
Two Wells
Gawler
Angaston
Lyndoch
N
ELIZABETH
St. Kilda
Mt. Pleasant
Outer Harbor
Birdwood
Tea Tree Gully
TO MANNUM
Port Adelaide
Lobethal
Grange Henley
ADELAIDE
TO KANGAROO ISLAND
Woodside
Glenelg
Brighton
Hahndorf
Reynella
Clarendon
Mount Barker
Christies Beach
TO MURRAY BRIDGE & MELBOURNE
GULF ST. VINCENT
McLaren Vale
Strathalbyn
Langhorne Creek
Normanville
Mount Compass
Goolwa
Victor Harbor
Cape Jervis
ENCOUNTER BAY

Getting there

The major domestic carriers, Ansett and Australian Airlines, serve Adelaide with non-stop daily flights to and from Sydney, Melbourne, Perth and Alice Springs, and regularly scheduled direct flights to and from Brisbane, Canberra, Darwin, the Gold Coast and Queensland's Sunshine Coast. Air time from Sydney is about 1 hour, 50 minutes; from Perth, it's about 3 hours. South Australian time is 30 minutes ahead of Sydney, Melbourne and Brisbane, but 1½ hours behind Western Australia. Several small carriers ply local routes; most notable is Kendall Airlines, which flies an Adelaide–Coober Pedy–Ayers Rock service every Saturday morning.

You can hire a vehicle and drive directly from Melbourne, 747 km (464 miles) via the Western and Dukes motorways, or Sydney, 1,433 km (890 miles) via the Mid Western and Stuart motorways. Brisbane is 2,056 km (1,277 miles) by the shortest route, Alice Springs is 1,697 km (1,054 miles), and if you're really adventurous, Perth is 2,720 km (1,690 miles) across the treacherous Nullarbor Plain. (Null arbor = 'no vegetation'.) Interstate buses ply these routes daily.

Rail service is also regular and efficient, with daily connections from Melbourne and Perth, six days a week from Sydney, and the famous 'Ghan' weekly from Alice Springs.

Getting around

You can hire a car at the airport or take the half-hourly Transit Regency coach into the city for A$2.40 (£1.15). Once you've arrived in Adelaide, the public transport system—called the *State Transport Authority* (12A Grenfell Street, tel. 210-1000)—will take good care of you. Buses run north to Elizabeth, south to Reynella, and east through the many communities of the Adelaide Hills. Suburban trains operate over a wider area, while the city's only electric tram links the city centre with the seaside suburb of Glenelg. The interconnecting services run from 6 a.m. to 11:30 p.m. Monday to Saturday, 9 a.m. to 10:30 p.m. Sunday. Fares start at 70 cents (33p). The *Adelaide Explorer Bus* (tel. 212-7344) stops at eight points on a 34-km (21-mile) circuit around the city; passengers who pay the A$6 (£2.85) adult fare can freely board and disembark over the course of the day.

Adelaide highlights

It makes sense for Adelaide visitors to focus their sightseeing attentions on **North Terrace**, the broad thoroughfare which demarcates the north end of the centre. On or near this street, you'll find the Adelaide Casino, Constitutional Museum, The Festival Centre, Government House, State Library, South

Australian Museum, Art Gallery of South Australia, University of
Adelaide, Ayers House and the Botanic Gardens—all within a
five-block stretch.
- The **South Australian Maritime Museum**, 119 Lipson
Street, Port Adelaide, has an enormous collection of marine
artifacts documenting South Australia's maritime history.
- **Glenelg** is Adelaide's most famous beach, a short trip from the
city centre by tram. Capt John Windmarsh landed here and
proclaimed the colony of South Australia in 1836; a replica of his
boat, the *HMS Buffalo*, contains restaurants and a museum.
Down the shore is a major amusement centre, Magic Mountain.
- **Carrick Hill**, 590 Fullarton Road, Springfield, a circa-1939
Elizabethan-style manor house surrounded by 96 acres of gardens
and bushland, contains a priceless private art collection of 19th
and 20th century oils, silver, pewter and furniture.
- ● ● The **Adelaide Hills** rise above the coastal plain 20
minutes' drive east of the city centre. Their charm is in their
views, bushland reserves and numerous unique villages scattered
through the gentle valleys. **Hahndorf**, 28 km (17 miles) from
Adelaide, was founded in 1839 by German refugees and is still
'sehr Deutsch': many original stone buildings house hotels,
restaurants and artisans' studios. **Birdwood Mill National
Motor Museum** at Birdwood has 300 vintage vehicles and other
antiques in an old flour mill. **Cleland Conservation Park**, on
the slopes of 2,333-foot Mount Lofty, is a great place for
bushwalking and for viewing native wildlife.

South Australia highlights
- ● ● The **Barossa Valley**—Is the largest wine-producing
district in Australia's major wine-producing state. Fifty separate
wineries, most of them located in a stretch of 23 km (14 miles)
along the Barossa Valley Highway between Lyndoch and
Nuriootpa, open their cellar doors daily for tastings of their
exquisite clarets and rieslings. The centre of the region is
Tanunda, a German town established in 1843 and the focus of
the Barossa Valley Vintage Festival, held in April of every odd-
numbered year (i.e. 1989, 1991).
- ● ● The **Flinders Ranges**—Comprise a majestic set of sharp
granite peaks and deep gorges 350 to 620 km (215 to 385 miles)
north of Adelaide. Within this wilderness are ancient Aboriginal
sites, abandoned mining towns, geological oddities, two national
parks (Flinders Ranges and Gammon) and the Wilpena Pound, an
enormous natural amphitheatre surrounded by steep cliffs.
- ● ● **Coober Pedy**—Is one of the world's most unusual communities. Most of the 2,100 residents of this opal-mining town,
943 km (586 miles) northwest of Adelaide by road, live in

underground 'dugouts' (homes) to escape the blistering desert heat. (The town's name derives from an Aboriginal phrase, 'kupa piti', meaning 'white man's hole'.) More than half the world's opals are mined at Coober Pedy. You can see demonstrations of opal cutting and polishing, or even get a budget bed, at the Umoona Mine; explore an underground display home and church, visit a museum, and shop for raw or cut opals. Coober Pedy is a good overnight stop between Adelaide and Alice Springs.

●● **Kangaroo Island**—Australia's third-largest offshore island, is best known for its plentiful wildlife. Some 150 km (90 miles) long, it is connected to Adelaide by four flights a day (A$84 (£40) return) and a daily ferry from Port Adelaide (A$29 (£13.80), leaving at 10 a.m., arriving at 11:30 a.m.). The main town Kingscote, is a farming centre, but the main visitor draw is Flinders Chase National Park, where kangaroos, koalas, emus and other native species run wild. Divers enjoy exploring offshore shipwrecks; fishing, bushwalking and sunning on the beaches are also popular.

●● The **Murray River** is Australia's 'Old Man River'. At 1,609 miles, it drains almost 1/7 of the Australian continent. Its final (and broadest) 400 miles cut through South Australia, emptying into Lake Alexandrina and Encounter Bay just south of Tailem Bend. You can cruise the river aboard a fully-contained paddle-wheeler like the *Proud Mary*, which sails between Murray Bridge and Renmark on 5-day or overnight cruises (33 Pirie Street, Adelaide; tel. 08/51-9472); or hire your own houseboat: contact the Lower Murray Regional Tourist Association, PO Box 344, Murray Bridge, SA 5253 (tel. 085/32-6660), for booking details.

Helpful hints

The **South Australian Government Travel Centre**, 18 King William Street near North Terrace (tel. 212-1644), operates a free information and booking service for hotels and tours throughout Adelaide and the state. It's open Monday to Friday 8:15 a.m. to 5:30 p.m., weekends and holidays 9 a.m. to 2 p.m.

PERTH AND WESTERN AUSTRALIA

Perth doesn't fit neatly into the main itinerary merely because of its isolation from the rest of Australia. Adelaide, some 2,200 km (1,400 miles) distant (by air), is the nearest city with more than 25,000 people, and Jakarta, Indonesia, is closer to Perth than the Australian national capital, Canberra.

For those with time, however, it's well worth a visit. Perth, where 1 million of the 1.4 million Western Australians live, is a lovely Mediterranean-style city nestled along the shores of the

broad Swan River. Best known in recent years as the temporary
(1983–1987) home of the America's Cup of yachting, Perth is the
gateway to a vast and varied state larger in itself than France.

Suggested schedule	
DAY 1	Arrive in Perth. Enjoy a walking tour of the city, from London Court to Kings Park.
DAY 2	Spend the day in Fremantle, an atmospheric European-style port town.
DAY 3	Cruise the Swan River, passing the Royal Perth Yacht Club and continuing to Rottnest Island, where you can bicycle among the quokkas.
DAY 4	Final sightseeing before an onward flight.

Getting there

Ansett and Australian Airlines have non-stop daily flights to Perth
from Adelaide, Melbourne and Sydney, and regular direct flights
from Brisbane, Cairns, Mount Isa, Alice Springs, Darwin and
Port Hedland. Air time from Sydney is about 4½ hours, from
Adelaide around 3 hours. (Perth time is 2 hours behind Sydney
and Melbourne, 1½ behind Adelaide and the Northern Territory.)
Think twice before driving across the seemingly endless Western
Australian desert to Perth. Taking the train, however, is a wise
alternative to flying. The 'Indian-Pacific' takes 66 hours from
Sydney, via Broken Hill, Adelaide and Kalgoorlie, three times a
week; the 'Trans-Australian' takes 38 hours from Adelaide (with
connections from Melbourne) twice a week.

Getting around

Hire a car at the airport, 11 km (7 miles) from the city centre,
take the Skybus coach to central Perth or major hotels for A$3.50
(£1.66), or catch a city bus. The public transport system, called
Transperth (125 St. George's Terrace, tel. 221-1211) operates
buses and trains weekly from 6 a.m. to 7:15 p.m., with reduced
service on weekends and holidays. Tickets good for two hours on
all services cost A$1 (47p). Free buses circle the city at 10-minute
intervals from 7 a.m. to 5:30 p.m. weekdays, 9 to 11:30 a.m.
Saturdays.

Perth sightseeing highlights

●● A walk down **St George's Terrace** offers a look at some of
Perth's most historic buildings, dating from the 1850s, plus some

unusual shopping arcades—notably **London Court**, reminiscent
of a quaint Elizabethan-era alley. Elsewhere in Perth, see:

● ● **Kings Park**, overlooking the west side of the city centre.
This 1,000-acre expanse, one of Australia's nicest city parks,
contains a botanical garden, a restaurant, numerous picnic
grounds, fountains and memorials, and some grand views across
Perth and the Swan River.

● The **Western Australian Museum**, Francis at Beaufort
Street, Northbridge (across the railway tracks from the centre).
It's interesting for its natural antiquities—an 11-ton meteorite, for
instance, and a 30-foot whale skeleton. It also has an Aboriginal
gallery, wildlife displays and the original 1856 Perth gaol.

● **The Art Gallery of Western Australia**, adjacent to the
museum on James Street at Beautfort, shares the Perth Cultural
Centre with the Alexander Library. The $10 million (£4.75
million) gallery has a superb permanent collection of Australian
(especially WA) and foreign works, among them Cezanne, Monet,
Picasso, Rembrandt, Renoir, Van Gogh and Whistler, plus a fine
display of tribal art and regional crafts.

● ● ● **Swan River cruises** leave from the Barrack Street Jetty at
the foot of the centre. **Transperth** offers a 2 p.m. upriver cruise
daily (returning at 4:45 p.m.) with an adult fare of A$8 (£3.80);
Captain Cook Cruises has three-hour daily cruises priced at
A$12 (£5.70), leaving at 1:45 p.m. daily; **Golden Swan Cruises**
offer full-day excursions to Fremantle for A$33 ((£15.70),
including lunch and sightseeing, or three-hour afternoon tea
cruises for A$12 (£5.70). A fourth operator with trips to
Fremantle and upriver to Swan Valley wineries is **Boat Torque
Cruises**. Your narrator will point out the Royal Perth Yacht
Club, the holder of the America's Cup from 1983 to 1987, and
the homes of many of the city's wealthier residents. You'll also
see a great many sailboards and other water sports: with no major
industry on the river, it is virtually without pollution.

● ● ● **Beaches** in Perth are among the finest in Australia. Long
strands of shimmering white sands extend from the Swan River
mouth at North Fremantle for many miles north. Best known,
from south to north, are **North Cottesloe**, Prince Charles'
personal favourite; **Swanbourne**, Perth's no. 1 nude beach; **City
Beach**, a family beach with modern facilities; and **Scarborough**,
site of the new $100 million (£47.5 million) Observation City
resort hotel complex.

● ● **Armadale**, a Perth suburb about 24 km (15 miles) south of
the city centre, is the home of **Pioneer World**, a recreated
working village of the late 19th century with various merchants
and tradesmen, a police station, fire station, general store, school-
house, theatre and a stream for gold panning. Nearby, you can

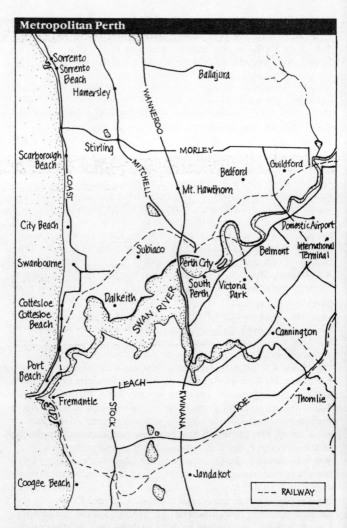

Metropolitan Perth

--- RAILWAY

regress a few more centuries at **The Elizabethan Village** containing replicas of Shakespeare's birthplace and other famous English buildings, plus antique weapons, armour, tapestries and furniture.

Fremantle sightseeing highlights

Western Australia's major port, settled in 1829, is situated at the mouth of the Swan River, just 19 km (12 miles) downstream from

Perth. At once more historic and more cosmopolitan than its 'big brother', it features many 19th century European-style buildings (more than 150 classified by the National Trust), an active and highly visible artisans' community, and of course its harbour and yachting marina. Fremantle is 35 minutes by Transperth train from downtown Perth; the one-way fare is 55 cents (25p).

●● **The Fremantle Museum and Arts Centre**, 1 Finnerty Street at Ord Street, is housed in a handsome stone building constructed in 1860 as a convict lunatic asylum. There are exhibits on the colonial history of Fremantle, the Swan River and the Western Australian coast, plus a fine display of local ceramics, sculpture, textiles, paintings and prints.

●● **The Western Australian Maritime Museum**, Cliff Street, exhibits artifacts of WA's rich trading and whaling history. Its star attraction is the *Batavia*, a Dutch sailing vessel shipwrecked in 1629 and now being reassembled timber by timber in the museum.

● The **America's Cup Museum**, 43 Swan Street, North Fremantle, has a collection of model yachts from the first America's Cup race through to the 1987 series, when the swiftest 12-metre sailing boats in the world made their homes in Fremantle for several months. The York Motor Museum of vintage cars is also at this address.

●● The **Round House**, on Arthur Head at the west end of High Street, is the state's oldest surviving building. Constructed in 1831 as the Swan River Colony's original civil gaol, it affords an excellent view across Fremantle and the harbour. Other convict-era structures include the grim-looking **Fremantle Gaol**, The Terrace (off Fairbairn Street), built by convicts between 1851 and 1859 and still used as a prison; and the **Warder's Quarters** on Henderson Street, stone terrace houses for prison guards and wardens.

● **Fremantle Markets**, South Terrace and Henderson Street, are a great place to browse for an 'arty' bargain or indulge in a variety of ethnic foods.

Rottnest Island

Perhaps the biggest surprise of many on this 5-by-11-km (3-by-7-mile) island, 18 km (11 miles) offshore from Fremantle, is that property developers haven't given it a new name. Its present monicker was provided by Dutch Commodore Willen de Vlamingh in 1696 when he mistook the native quokkas, miniature kangaroos, for rats. Developed in the 1830s as a convict farm colony, it was converted to minor resort status in 1917. The **Rottnest Museum**, housed in the 1857 grain-crushing mill, will tell you about the island's historic cottages and natural history.

The **Underwater Explorer**, a semi-submersible submarine, offers cruises to look at shipwrecks, marine life and reef formations. But the best way to see the island is to hire a bicycle from **Rottnest Bike Hire**, just behind the Hotel Rottnest, and pay A\$5 (£2.35) to pedal around for half a day. (There are no cars on the island.) Visit the salt lakes with their rich bird life, Second World War gun emplacements, a lighthouse on the island's highest point, and impressive sandy beaches inviting you for a swim. You're almost sure to see the friendly little quokkas: the entire island is a wildlife sanctuary.

Get to Rottnest aboard the M/V *Temeraire II* from Barracks Street Jetty in Perth (\$18 (£8.50) same-day return) or Fremantle (A\$14 (£6.66) return). It's about a 1½-hour ride from Perth. **Boat Torque Cruises** also operate daily package cruises, leaving Perth daily at 9 a.m. (returning at 5:45 p.m.) for A\$37 to \$42 (£17.60 to £20), including lunch at Rottnest and a two-hour bus tour of the island. By air, it's A\$19 (£9) return to Rottnest from the Perth Flight Centre at Perth airport, or A\$25 (£12) return on the *Island Hopper* helicopter from the Port Beach Road terminal in North Fremantle. Several lodgings are available on the island.

Highlights of Western Australia

Western Australia is Australia's largest state, sprawling across 965,000 square miles from the tropical Kimberley to the forests and meadows of the southwest. Most of it is foreboding desert and stark terrain suitable for miners and kangaroos. But there are numerous areas of tourist interest for those with the time and the inclination.

●● **The Southwest** is the state's most fertile region. Besides its orchards, vineyards and cattle farms, there are surfing beaches and limestone caves along the west coast, forests of karri trees (300 feet high, 23 feet around) near Pemberton, the startling bluffs of the **Stirling Range National Park**, and the famous **Wave Rock** near Hyder. The largest towns are **Albany** (pop. 22,000), a beach town and agricultural centre; and **Esperance** (pop. 7,000) gateway to the Archipelago of the Recherche, famous among divers. Australians flock to the Southwest in droves between August and November, when spring speckles the meadows and mountain slopes with 8,000 varieties of colourful wildflowers.

●● **The Goldfields** district focuses on **Kalgoorlie** (pop. 25,000), centre of the state's gold-mining industry, 597 km (371 miles) east of Perth. Not quite a century ago, some 200,000 hopeful 'diggers' worked this desert region seeking their fortunes. Kalgoorlie's wide streets and false-fronted hotels today are reminders of the gold-rush era. Travellers visit the Hainault

Tourist Mine to learn past and modern gold-mining methods, both under and above ground. Brothels, not legal, are tolerated here. Most of the nearby towns built in the decade following the 1893 discovery of gold—like Gwalia, Broad Arrow and Menzies— are now ghost towns. Alone among them, **Coolgardie** has been preserved as a living monument to the era, although its population has shrunk from 15,000 to 900. Don't miss the **Goldfields Museum**, open daily.

●● **The Midlands** include numerous fascinating attractions within a day's drive north and east of Perth. **The Pinnacles**, calcified spires of an ancient forest 30,000 years old, are in Nambung National Park. **New Norcia** is a fragment of medieval Spain, complete with a Benedictine monastery and an astounding museum and art gallery. **York** is the historical (1840s) centre of the agriculturally rich Avon Valley.

● **The North Coast** starts at **Geraldton** (pop. 21,000), a farming and lobster-fishing centre 423 km (263 miles) north of Perth. Many famous shipwrecks, including the 1629 *Batavia* disaster, occurred in the Abrolhos isles offshore. A short distance north is the self-proclaimed **Principality of Hutt**, where Prince Leonard, a former farmer with his tongue firmly in cheek, even issues his own postage stamps. **Kalbarri National Park** features some spectacular gorges on the Murchison River. **Carnarvon** (pop. 5,000), 801 km (498 miles) from Perth, is famous for its banana farms and prawning. **Port Hedland** (pop. 12,000), 1,547 km (978 miles) from Perth on Highway 1, is the principal port for the Pilbara, Australia's major iron ore region. At nearby Marble Bar, temperatures once exceeded 100 degrees Fahrenheit for five straight months.

●● **The Kimberley** is a remote, rugged region best seen during the cool, dry winter season (May to August). **Geikie Gorge**, on the Fitzroy River, and **Windjana Gorge**, on the Meda, are the most remarkable of several grandiose chasms in the King Leopold Ranges. **Tunnel Creek** has gouged a half-mile natural tunnel through limestone. The indented coastline is notable for its prolific crop of crocodiles! (Tourists beware: An American woman was gobbled alive in 1987.) **Broome** (pop. 4,000), 2,151 km (1,337 miles) from Perth, is a former pearl-diving centre which has shifted its economic base to cultured pearls. Its blend of Europeans with third-generation Japanese, Malays and other Asians is unique in Australia. Northeast of the Kimberley, **Kununurra** (pop. 2,500), 3,140 km (1,951 miles) from Perth, was founded in 1960 as a base for the massive Ord River Irrigation Scheme. Water sports and cruises are popular on Lake Argyle, WA's biggest inland body of water. A large diamond mine opened near here in 1985 after a major deposit was discovered.

Helpful hints
The **Western Australian Tourism Commission** has its offices
at 16 St George's Terrace, Perth (tel. 220-1700). For everyday
tourism information and bookings, visit the **Holiday WA Centre**
at 772 Hay Street in Perth (322-2999) or 4 High Street in
Fremantle (tel. 430-5555).

DARWIN AND THE 'TOP END'

The main reason to go to Australia's 'Top End'—the northern
crown of the Northern Territory—is to visit Kakadu National
Park. If you saw *Crocodile Dundee* and savoured the fantastic
wetland wilderness in which most of the Australian segment of
the movie was filmed, you know just what Kakadu looks like.
You even saw Jabiru, Mick Dundee's 'home town', near which
the park headquarters are located.

Darwin, the gateway to Kakadu, is the hard-drinking capital of
the Northern Territory. It has survived Japanese bombing in 1942
and a devastating cyclone in 1974 to become an interesting
cosmopolitan city of 65,000.

Your schedule in the 'Top End' should allow you a day in
Darwin, as much time as you can make available in Kakadu, and
possible side trips to Katherine Gorge and/or the Aboriginal communities on Bathurst or Melville islands. Keep in mind, though,
that the oppressively humid wet season, from late November to
March, is probably not a good time to visit.

Getting there
There are direct daily flights to Darwin from Adelaide, Brisbane,
Melbourne, Perth and Sydney aboard Ansett, Ansett WA or
Australian Airlines, and additional direct flights (not daily) from
Cairns, Mount Isa and Port Hedland. Air time from Alice
Springs is 1 hour, 50 minutes; from Sydney 4 hours; from Perth
(with one stop) 4½ hours. Ansett NT offers non-stop flights
several times a week to and from Katherine, Tennant Creek and
Gove/Nhulunbuy in the Northern Territory. There are also
international connections to Indonesia and Singapore.

There's no train service to Darwin, but you can travel overland
by private car—a gruelling effort, not recommended—or by
express coach. No doubt the cheapest way to reach Darwin from
major population centres is with an unlimited-mileage bus pass
from Ansett Pioneer, Greyhound or Deluxe Coaches. From Alice
Springs, buses normally take 21 hours (overnight) and charge
A$107 (£50).

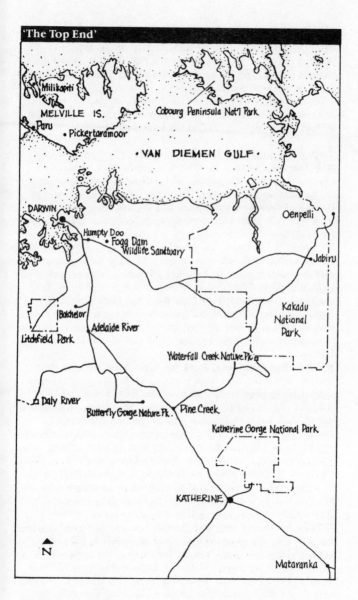

'The Top End'

Milikapiti
MELVILLE IS.
Paru
Pickertaramoor
Cobourg Peninsula Nat'l Park
VAN DIEMEN GULF
DARWIN
Oenpelli
Humpty Doo
Fogg Dam
Wildlife Sanctuary
Jabiru
Kakadu National Park
Batchelor
Adelaide River
Litchfield Park
Waterfall Creek Nature Pk.
Daly River
Butterfly Gorge Nature Pk.
Pine Creek
Katherine Gorge National Park
KATHERINE
N
Mataranka

Getting around

From Darwin airport, 6 km from town, you can hire a car, take
an A$8 (£3.80) taxi ride, or hop on the airport shuttle bus for a

A$2.50 (£1.20) ride into the city centre. Within the city, public
buses (tel. 81-2150) operate 6 a.m. to 11 p.m., Monday to
Saturday, at a cost of 30 cents (14p) a ride. You can also hire
bicycles for A$5 (£2.40) a day at **City Cycle Rental**, 69 Mitchell
Street in the Greyhound depot.

You can take a long-distance coach to Katherine, but to
Arnhem Land or the offshore Aboriginal reserves, your best bet is
to book a company tour, of which several are available.

Top End sightseeing highlights

● ● **Darwin**, founded in 1869, was named after naturalist
Charles Darwin by the captain of HMS *Beagle*, who discovered
the harbour 30 years earlier. The main sights include the
Botanical Gardens, established in 1891 and now containing
more than 400 species of tropical plants on 85 acres; **Doctor's
Gully**, where thousands of ocean fish come in at high tide daily
for a free feed of bread; the **Northern Territory Museum of
Arts and Natural Sciences**, notable for its primitive art and
wildlife exhibits; and the **Artillery Museum**, with reminders of
Darwin's World War Two buffeting. If you're up here in June,
don't miss the annual **Beer Can Regatta.** Darwinites, who
consume an average of 60 gallons of beer per year for every man,
woman and child, save up their empty cans for 51 weeks in order
to construct an imaginative flotilla that sets sail on Darwin
Harbour.

● ● ● **Kakadu National Park** has been called the greatest
wetland remaining on Planet Earth. Over 2,300 square miles in
area, it comprises the floodplains of the East, South and West
Alligator Rivers and the Wildman River, and the sudden cliffs of
the Arnhem Land escarpment with gorges, waterfalls and
18,000-year-old Aboriginal rock paintings. Join a safari for one to
eight days of bushwalking, camping and cruising the rivers. Book
a trip from Darwin with **Terra Safari Tours**, 1585 Strath Road,
Berrimah, NT (tel. 089/84-3470); **Australian Kakadu Tours**,
PO Box 1397, Darwin (tel. 81-5144); or **Dial-a-Safari**, 14
Knucky Street, Darwin (tel. 81-1244). Costs average around
A$100 (£48) a day.

● ● **Bathurst and Melville Islands**, traditional homes of the
isolated Tiwi Aboriginal tribes, are situated 80 km (50 miles)
north of Darwin across the Clarence Strait. Tiwi pottery and
woodcarvings, especially ceremonial grave poles, are unique.
Contact **Tiwi Tours**, 27 Temira Crescent, Darwin (tel. 81-5115)
to book a highly worthwhile half-day (A$125 (£60)) or full-day
(A$185 (£88)) tour between March and October.

● ● **Katherine Gorge National Park**, 31 km (19 miles) from
Katherine (pop. 4,500) and 388 km (241 miles) southeast of

Darwin, is best known for its boat trips between the sheer, 200-foot-high walls of the chasm. Two-hour cruises run four times daily the rest of the year, for about A$10 (£4.75) adult fare.

Helpful hints

You'll find the helpful **Northern Territory Government Tourist Bureau** at 31 Smith Street Mall (tel. 81-6611), open 8:45 a.m. to 5 p.m. Monday to Friday and 9 a.m. to noon Saturday.

GREAT BARRIER REEF ISLANDS

If a visit to Green Island (Tour 17) whets your appetite for more time in the tropical sun, you'll be pleased to know that there are hundreds of other islands off the coast of Queensland between the Gold Coast and Cape Melville, spread across 1,300 km (800 miles) of South Pacific Ocean. Nearly two dozen of them have established resort settlements.

Getting there

The main gateway towns are Bundaberg, Gladstone, Rockhampton, Mackay, Proserpine, Townsville, Cardwell, Tully, Cairns and Cooktown, scattered up the coast north of Brisbane. All are connected by highway; all but Cooktown are linked via rail; all but Cardwell and Tully have domestic airports of their own.

Once you've reached the gateway town, it's a relatively painless procedure to get to the islands by boat (every resort has its own launch service from nearby mainland harbours) or small plane. Inquire locally for directions or check with the nearest Queensland Government Travel Centre.

The busiest gateway town is **Proserpine**, the take-off point for the Whitsunday Islands. Located 1,165 (724 miles) north of Brisbane and 650 km (404 miles) south of Cairns, it is served by non-stop flights from Brisbane, Townsville and Mackay several times a week, and by direct flights (with stops) from Sydney and Melbourne. Coaches connect Proserpine with Shute Harbour, 22 km (14 miles) east, from which launches run several times daily to the various resorts of the Whitsundays.

Island highlights

Every Barrier Reef island has something a little different to offer the visitor. Some are upmarket, jet-set resorts, with all manner of sports facilities and nightlife. Others are limited to rustic cottages or youth hostel accommodation. You're bound to find something to match your desires and price range.

The following listing singles out major resort islands (except for those covered in our Cairns itinerary), starting in the south and moving north:

Lady Elliot Island is the southernmost coral cay on the reef. Visitors come to this tiny isle to enjoy the marine life with tank, snorkel or on foot at low tide. Full board lodging costs A\$55 to \$75 (£26 to £36) in scattered cabins or safari tents. There's no launch service; charter aircraft from Bundaberg charge A\$95 (£45) return.

Heron Island is famous worldwide for its outstanding scuba diving and snorkelling. Just 42 acres in area, this unspoiled cay is surrounded by over 9 square miles of coral reef. The Barrier Reef Divers Festival is held every November; the rest of the year, you can get excellent diving instruction and equipment. In addition to the reef life, you can see green sea turtles and migratory mutton birds nest here (the island is a national park) and lay their eggs in spring and summer. Launches leave Gladstone daily except Thursday at 8 a.m., arriving at Heron Island (a distance of 72 km, or 45 miles) 2½ hours later, for A\$100 (£48) return. Or you can take a helicopter for A\$217 (£103) return.

Great Keppel Island is as frantic as Heron and Lady Elliot are serene. The largest of 27 mostly-undeveloped islands in the Keppel Group, 13 km (8 miles) east of Yeppoon, near Rockhampton, it is heavily geared toward singles in their 20s. At the main resort, activities are scheduled every minute of the day and night, from water sports to disco dancing (there's a resident rock band), tennis and golf to squash and cricket. The resort is owned by Australian Airlines, which offers weekly packages. To get to Great Keppel, take a coach from Rockhampton to Rosslyn Bay (near Yeppoon), then pay A\$12 (£5.70) return for the hydrofoil. There are also several 25-minute flights daily from Rockhampton.

Brampton Island, 32 km (20 miles) north of Mackay, is a national park and wildlife sanctuary. The mountainous, 1,100-acre island is cloaked in tropical forest and surrounded by white sand beaches and coral reefs. It's great for bushwalking among semi-tame kangaroos and colourful lorikeets. At Brampton Island Resort, an Australian Airlines hotel, activities include all manner of water sports, tennis and golf, and a disco for nightlife. Launch service operates daily from Mackay at 9 a.m. The cruise takes an hour, and the cost is A\$24 (£11.50) return. If you prefer to fly, Air Queensland makes the short hop from Mackay.

Newry Island, a hilly, wooded national park of just 110 acres, is one of the least known (and most un-touristy) of all the isles off the Queensland coast. Koalas and echidnas are native to the island, a good place for walking and swimming. A small resort accommodates 25 guests; camping is also available. A launch service operates from Victor Creek, 56 km (35 miles) north of

Mackay, at 11:00 a.m. every Wednesday, Saturday and Sunday. It takes 15 minutes; the fare is A$10 (£4.75).

Lindeman Island is on the southern fringe of the Whitsunday Group, 74 islands discovered and named by Captain Cook in 1770. Lindeman was the first of the Barrier Reef resorts, established in 1929 and still a favourite for many Australian families. Walking trails climb the hills of this rocky, 2000-acre isle. There are organised activities for kids of all ages. Launch fare from Shute Harbour is A$20 (£9.50) return; flights from Proserpine are A$60 (£28.50) return.

Hamilton Island is the luxurious, world-class resort centre of the Whitsundays. The A$200 million (£95 million) hotel complex features five restaurants and a French bakery, seven bars (including one of the swim-up variety in Australia's largest freshwater pool), an indoor sports complex, a shopping centre with four boutiques, a 200-acre fauna park, a 400-boat marina, sport fishing charters and scuba diving instruction, and a 'floating hotel', the Coral Cat, hovering above the reef. The 1,200-acre island is quite hilly, but there's enough flat ground for Queensland's only island airport where large jets can land. Ansett flies non-stop daily from Cairns and several times weekly from Brisbane, Sydney and Melbourne. A 45-minute launch service runs twice daily (9 a.m. and 4:45 p.m.) from Shute Harbour for a return fare of A$25 (£12).

Long Island has two very different resort communities about 2 km apart. The Ansett-owned Whitsunday 100 Resort competes for the 18-to-35 singles clientele of Great Keppel Island with non-stop water sports by day, disco dancing by night. A$85 to $90 (£40.50 to £43) per person. Budget travellers, meanwhile, enjoy Palm Bay Resort, cook their own food (there's a small grocery) and enjoy bush walking and snorkelling. Long Island is a lush national park 11 km (7 miles) long, no more than 1½ km wide, and everywhere mountainous. Launches run four times daily (9 a.m. to 4:45 p.m.) from Shute Harbour, 8 km (5 miles) northwest. The round-trip fare is A$16 (£7.50) to Palm Bay, A$20 (£9.50) to Whitsunday 100.

South Molle Island is a 1,000-acre island of steep bush-covered hills and coral-fringed bays in the heart of the Whitsunday Passage. A national park, it is criss-crossed by walking tracks and inhabited by brightly coloured lorikeets. The medium-sized resort offers water sports, fishing, gymnasium, golf and tennis. It is served by restaurants, bars and other facilities. Launch service from Shute Harbour (daily at 9 a.m., 1 and 5 p.m.) costs A$20 (£9.50) return.

Daydream Island is tiny, just ¾ of a mile long and barely 500 metres (547 yards) wide. Social life on this speck of paradise,

clutched by white coral beaches and lazy coconut palms, focuses
on the resort's huge lagoon-style swimming pool with its bar on a
central island (no 'dry' martinis here). There are the usual variety
of water and other sports, and a disco for the night-time. The
island is served twice daily (9 a.m. and 5 p.m.) by launch from
Shute Harbour, 5 km (3 miles) distant, for A$15 (£7) return.

Hayman Island, one of the oldest of the Reef resorts (it dates
from the 1950s), was reincarnated in 1986 as a five-star resort
after a A$100 million (£47.5 million) renovation by Ansett. It's a
universally appealing island with 1,000 acres of rugged mountain
scenery, a wide fringe of reef, palm-shaded beaches, and dozens of
species of birds and butterflies. The Ansett International Hotel
has five restaurants, a library, a lively entertainment centre and
fine water sports facilities. If you aren't in the mood for a cruise
boat from Shute Harbour (A$25 (£12) return), you can fly by
helicopter from Proserpine or direct by Turbo Beaver from Airlie
Beach (near Shute Harbour) or Townsville.

Magnetic Island is almost a suburb of Townsville. Just 13 km
(8 miles) north of Queensland's third largest city, it attracts
hundreds or even thousands of day trippers. But it's big
enough—20 square miles—that the throngs are easily escaped.
Another mountainous national park island, it has fine bush
walking, a fernery and an aquarium, bird and koala sanctuaries,
two dozen sandy beaches and a motor road linking several resort
villages along the eastern shore. (The island even has its own bus
service.) You can hire bicycles or mopeds at Picnic Bay, where
the ferry arrives 8 to 12 times daily from Townsville (35 minutes,
A$6 (£2.85) return). The island contains at least half a dozen
official and unofficial youth hostels, numerous holiday flats and
economy-priced hotels in Picnic Bay and Arcadia. Australian
Airlines' Alma Dean Beach Resort midway up the east coast is a
top resort.

Orpheus Island is one of the more secluded of the reef resorts,
80 km (50 miles) northwest of Townsville and 24 km (15 miles)
east of Lucinda, near Ingham. Eleven km (7 miles) long, not quite
a mile wide, and fringed with reef, the forested island—volcanic
in origin—is a national park rich in birdlife and turtle nesting
grounds. There's no regular launch service, but seaplanes or
helicopters operate daily from Townsville for A$155 (£74) return.

Hinchinbrook Island is the world's largest island national park,
a 144-square-mile Tahitian landscape of lush rain forest, mist-
shrouded mountains (up to 3,400 feet high), spectacular waterfalls, rocky caves, sandy beaches (on the east coast) and rich
wildlife. A narrow channel separates it from the mainland east of
Cardwell, about halfway between Townsville and Cairns.
Launches leave Cardwell daily except Monday at 9 a.m., with a

fare of A\$24 (£11.50) return.

Bedarra Island is a tiny and exclusive resort island. One mile long and a half-mile wide, four miles off the coast near Tully, it is densely forested and ringed by white sandy beaches. The new Bedarra Bay Resort consists of two dozen elaborate guest bungalows set in a tropical garden along the ocean. There's no organised entertainment of any type—nothing but 'intimate, casual and elegant' relaxation, as promoters put it. No one under 15 is allowed. Reach Bedarra aboard a daily launch service via Dunk Island from Clump Point, near Tully (A\$18 (£8.50) return).

Dunk Island is another unspoiled gem with a remarkably rich fauna and flora. Lush jungle caresses the slopes of 900-foot Mount Koo-tal-oo, providing a home for some 150 species of birds, plus dozens of beetles and butterflies, lizards and snakes, bats and echidnas. The island is only 520 acres in size, but it somehow seems larger. Sophisticated over-30s like its Great Barrier Reef Hotel, which offers all the sports of other island resorts plus horse riding, skeet shooting and nature activities. Get there on a launch from Clump Point, 5 km (3 miles) west, for A\$12 (£5.75) return; water taxi from South Mission Beach; or a flight with Australian Airlines (the resort owner) daily from Townsville and several times a week from Cairns.

Lizard Island is the northernmost of the Barrier Reef resort islands, 95 km (59 miles) northeast of Cooktown. Situated close to the magnificent outer reef, this lovely 4-square-mile island has great beaches, better snorkelling, and some of the world's finest big-game fishing within easy cast. Lizard Island Lodge is an exclusive resort overlooking a coral lagoon. Air Queensland flies to Lizard Island at least once a day from Cairns (A\$96 (£46)) or Cooktown (A\$58 (£28)).

Helpful hints

Queensland Government Travel Centres are situated in three towns between Brisbane and Cairns: Rockhampton (119 East Street, tel. 079/27-8611); Mackay (River Street, tel. 079/57-2292); and Townsville (303 Flinders Mall, tel. 077/71-3077). The QGTC's main office is at 196 Adelaide Street, Brisbane, Qld 4000 (tel. 07/31-2211). Most of the reef resorts have postal services and shops; many also have banking facilities and resident medical practitioners.

HOLIDAYS & FESTIVALS

January
New Year's Day (1st)
Australia Day (1st Monday after Jan. 26)
Surfing carnivals (throughout beach communities until March)

February
Festival of Perth (1st three weeks)

March
Moomba Festival, Melbourne (10 days early in month)
Festival of Arts, Adelaide (even-numbered years)
Hunter Valley Vintage Festival, New South Wales
Sheffield Shield Final, national cricket championship

April
Barossa Vintage Festival, South Australia, odd-numbered years
Festival of the Rocks, Sydney (week before Easter)
Good Friday and Easter Sunday (dates vary)
Royal Agricultural Show, Sydney (Easter week)
ANZAC Day (25th)

May
Bangtail Muster, Alice Springs (1st weekend)

June
Beer Can Regatta, Darwin (1st weekend)
Townsville Pacific Festival (11 days in early June)
Queen's Birthday (2nd Monday, except in WA)

July
Lots of footy and horse races, if nothing else

August
Brisbane Royal Show (middle of month)
Shinju Matsuri, Broome, WA (3rd to 4th weekend)
Henley-on-Todd Regatta, Alice Springs (last Saturday)
Australian Ski Championships, Thredbo

September
Royal Adelaide Show (early in month)
Melbourne Royal Agricultural Show (middle of month)
Spoleto Festival of Arts, Melbourne (last two weeks)
Warana Spring Carnival, Brisbane (last two weeks)
Victorian Football League Grand Final, Melbourne (4th Saturday)

October
Perth Royal Show (early in month)
Queen's Birthday (1st Monday, WA only)
Tropicarnival, Gold Coast (2nd week)
Royal Hobart Show (3rd weekend)
Australian Formula 1 Grand Prix, Adelaide (end of month)

November
Melbourne Cup horse race (1st Tuesday)
Australian Open Golf Tournament (3rd weekend)

December
Christmas and Boxing Day (Dec. 25 and 26)
Sydney-to-Hobart Yacht Race (starting Dec. 26)

HOW TO SPEAK 'STRINE'

Yes, Australians do speak English—but it often seems to be a
different English language from what most of us are used to
hearing. For starters, the dialect is a bit odd, with the long 'A'
sounding more like an 'I' and the 'R', except at the beginning of
a word, often dropped altogether. Once you become accustomed
to that, you find that there's a whole new vocabulary you never
learned in school. The following list is an attempt to make your
understanding a bit easier.

'Strine', by the way, was one foreigner's attempt to transliterate
the word 'Australian' as it is sometimes pronounced.

amber beer
arvo afternoon
Aussie what an Australian calls himself
back of beyond the outback
back of Bourke way out in the outback
Banana bender native Queenslander
barbie barbecue
barrack cheer the team to victory
battler a persistent person
bent drunk or stoned
billabong water hole in an intermittent river
billy tin pot used to boil water for tea
bitumen surfaced road
blowfly the Australian national pest
blue fight
bo peep quick look
bonzer wonderful
boomer very large; especially, a large kangaroo
bottle shop off-licence
bowser petrol pump; also, tanker truck
brumby wild horse
Buckley's chance a snowball's chance in hell
Bullamakanka beyond the back of Bourke
bush anything outside a town or city
bushranger 19th century outlaw
bushwalking hiking
chook chicken
cobber mate
come a gutser make a bad mistake
come the raw prawn be deceitful
coolabah a type of eucalyptus tree
corroboree Aboriginal festival
crook sick, broken or no good

cut lunch   sandwiches
daks   trousers
damper   unleavened bread (bush tucker)
didgeridoo   Aboriginal musical instrument; it drones
digger   originally a gold miner; later a soldier; now, often, any
Australian
dingo   native wild dog
dinkie die   fair dinkum
dinkum   honest, genuine
do your block   lose your temper
drongo   born loser, ne'er-do-well
dunny   outhouse
Enzed   New Zealand
evo   evening
fair dinkum   the complete, honest truth
flake   shark meat (used in fish and chips)
footy   Australian football
g'day   universal greeting
galah   rose-coloured parrot; also, a fool
get off your bike   become angry
give it a burl   give it a try
give it the flick   get rid of it
going troppo   moving to the far north
goodonya   'Good on you', 'Way to go'.
grazier   livestock rancher with large holdings
greenies   environmentalists
hang a Louie   do a left turn
hang a Roscoe   Do a right turn
hard case   enjoyable person to be around
have on   accept a challenge; also, pull one's leg
hump   root; also, to carry (as a swag)
jackeroo   apprentice cowboy
jilleroo   apprentice cowgirl
jumbuck   sheep
kip   bed
lob   arrive
lolly water   soda pop
matilda   belongings carried in a swag
middy   medium-sized glass of beer
milk bar   corner grocery
Moreton Bay bug   a small yabbie (freshwater crayfish)
Never Never   desert land, inhabited by Aboriginals
outback   unsettled bush
Oz   Australia
penguin   nun
peter   cash register

Pom   Englishman
prang   crash or dent
rage   party
ripper   great!
roo   kangaroo
roos in his paddock   bats in his belfry
'scuse I   excuse me
sea wasp   jellyfish with highly potent venom
sealed   tarmacked (as in a road)
Seppo   American (from rhyming slang: Yank = Septic Tank = Seppo)
sheila   young woman
shoot through   leave suddenly
silk shirt on a pig   something wasted
silver beet   spinach
silvertail   member of high society
sly grogger   after-hours drinking establishment
smoke-o   tea break
snag   sausage
sprog   baby
spunky   sexy-looking
station   large farm or ranch in the Outback
stickybeak   busybody
stockman   ranch hand
Strine   Aussie lingo
swag   small bundle of personal belongings
swagman   hobo
Sydney or the bush   all or nothing
takeaway bar   fast-food restaurant
Tazzie   Tasmania
track   outback road
tube   can of beer
tucker   food
two-pot screamer   person unable to hold their beer
uni (or varsity)   university
up a gum tree   in a dilemma
ute   utility truck; pickup truck
walkabout   travelling on foot for a long way without a specific destination
walloper   policeman
wasted   drunk
wharfie   longshoreman
witchety grubs   sweet worms, cooked in sauce
yabber   chatter
yabbie   freshwater crayfish (small lobster)
yakka   work